SHE TAKES A STAND

SHE TAKES A STAND

16 FEARLESS ACTIVISTS WHO HAVE CHANGED THE WORLD

MICHAEL ELSOHN ROSS

CHICAGO
REVIEW
PRESS

Copyright © 2015 by Michael Elsohn Ross
All rights reserved
Published by Chicago Review Press, Incorporated
814 North Franklin Street
Chicago, Illinois 60610

ISBN 978-1-61373-026-3

Interior design: Sarah Olson

Library of Congress Cataloging-in-Publication Data

Ross, Michael Elsohn, 1952–
  She takes a stand : 16 fearless activists who have changed the world / Michael
Elsohn Ross.
     pages cm. — (Women of action)
  Summary: "Portraits of brave women from the late 1800s through today—
role models who are passionate about important issues   A source of
inspiration for young women with strong social convictions, She Takes a Stand
highlights 16 extraordinary women who have fought for human rights, civil
rights, workers' rights, reproductive/sexual rights, and world peace. Among
these are many who have been imprisoned, threatened, or suffered financial
hardships for pursuing their missions to change the world for the better.
Included are historic heroes such as anti-lynching crusader Ida B. Wells and
suffragist Alice Paul, along with contemporary figures such as girls-education
activist Malala Yousafzai; "Gulabi Gang" founder Sampat Pal Devi, who fights
violence against Indian women; and SPARK executive director Dana Edell,
who works to end the sexualization of women and girls in the media. Taking
a multicultural, multinational perspective, She Takes a Stand spotlights brave
women around the world with an emphasis on childhood details, motivations,
and life turning points—in many cases gleaned from the author's original
interviews—and includes related sidebars, a bibliography, source notes, and
a list of organizations young women can explore to get involved in changing
their world"— Provided by publisher.
  Includes bibliographical references and index.
  ISBN 978-1-61373-026-3 (hardback)
  1. Women social reformers—Juvenile literature. 2. Women political
activists—Juvenile literature. 3. Women's rights—Juvenile literature. 4.
Women—Political activity—Juvenile literature. I. Title.

HQ1236.R5965 2015
320.082—dc23

                              2015001401

Printed in the United States of America
5 4 3 2 1

To my dear friend Lynn MacMichael,
a devoted activist for peace and justice,
who has inspired me to write this book.

CONTENTS

PART III: REJECTING VIOLENCE

INTRODUCTION

———◆———

SEARCHING FOR SUPERHEROES

When citizens are faced with villains in comic books and movies, a superhero arrives in the nick of time to set things right. In the real world, it takes ordinary people doing the extraordinary to confront violence and injustice. Normal people rising up to change the world for the better are as courageous as any superhero.

Among these heroes are girls and women who have reached the point where they feel they have no choice but to take action. In this book you will meet 16 such women, young and old, from all over the world—like Kalpona Akter, a girl fired from her job in a garment factory for trying to improve horrid working conditions, and Ida B. Wells, a young black reporter who set out, armed only with her words, to end the lynchings of African Americans. Each of them found the courage and perseverance to pursue her goals for as long as it took, despite threats against their lives. Other activists, such as musician Buffy Sainte-Marie and painter Judy Baca, chose to use their artistic talents in service of social change.

These stories and those of 12 other courageous women may inspire you to take action to solve a problem, whether it is in your neighborhood or the global community, and become one more ordinary person accomplishing one more extraordinary act.

MEGAN GRASSELL

———◆———

Ripening a Yellowberry

---

*"One of the biggest problems I had getting started was getting
people to take me and my ideas seriously."* — Megan Grassell

---

n the following pages you will meet women who have taken
a stand for basic rights and respect, against greed and corruption, and against violence around the world. But sometimes a practical problem in your own family can prompt you
to act. That's what happened to Megan Grassell, an inspiring
example of how one teen got fired up and wouldn't *give* up. Her
efforts now contribute to the comfort and emotional well-being
of thousands of young teen and tween girls.

Megan was born on August 16, 1995, in Jackson Hole, Wyoming. Her father, Chopper, grew up in the Green River Valley
of Wyoming. Her mother, Lynn, was from Georgia. Grandma
Susan, Chopper's mother, was raised on a ranch lacking both
electricity and running water. In this rugged rural area many
people learn to be resourceful and, though independent in spirit,
are always ready to lend a hand.

Megan during her senior
year of high school.
Courtesy of Megan Grassell

Growing up in the small town of Pinedale, on the west side of the Wind River Mountains, Megan enjoyed fun times outdoors with her older brother Will.

Megan's carefree days with Will and their younger sister, Caroline, nicknamed Buggs, didn't last long. When Megan was in kindergarten Will was diagnosed with brain cancer. Fortunately, after treatment, he was cancer free. But then, just a month before Megan's seventh birthday, Caroline fell off a float in the Rendezvous Parade, and she died as a result, a tragic loss for the family and community. Later their mother gave birth to another daughter, Mary Margaret.

After her sister Caroline's abrupt death, Megan focused on taking life slower and savoring each moment. Caroline's godparents had written some simple mantras to celebrate Caroline's life: "Water the flowers every day, Watch quietly and observe, Go barefoot, Love the outdoors and nature, Seek and find a hug when you need one, and finally, Campfires are rare, eat as many marshmallows as you can." These became guiding principles for Megan.

With its pigs, lambs, chickens, goats, cattle, and horses, their home was like a small farm. All of the Grassell kids grew up camping, skiing, and riding horses. Megan placed first in rodeo events such as barrel racing and pole bending. She also enjoyed competing in downhill skiing races. When Megan needed money, she knew that her parents expected her to work for it. "I worked every summer since sixth or seventh grade. First pumping gas and then I bussed tables and waitressed at a place called Nora's." Just before the start of eighth grade, Megan and her family moved to nearby Jackson Hole.

At the age of 17 a shopping trip with her mom to help 13-year-old sister Mary Margaret buy her first bra changed Megan's path in life. "I couldn't believe the bras that she was supposed to buy. The choices for her, and for all girls her age, were simply appalling to me. They were all padded, push-up, and sexual. Not only that, they did not fit her body properly, which automatically made me wonder, 'Where were the young, cute, and realistic bras for girls?' There were none!" recalled Megan in a magazine interview.

At that moment Megan decided she would make bras for girls. It didn't matter that Megan knew so little about sewing that she didn't even know how to patch a pair of pants—or that she had to come up with a design, figure out where to manufacture the bras, and learn how to sell them. Megan knew how to ask for help.

She chose to name her company Yellowberry to highlight her belief that young girls shouldn't be pushed into growing up too fast. They didn't need to wear sexy adult bras or padded bras to make them look older. Like a yellow berry, they were still "ripening." In their transition between childhood and adulthood, they needed a bra that was fun and comfortable.

One step at a time, Megan moved toward making her bras a reality. A local seamstress in Jackson Hole helped her create prototypes, which young friends helped her test for comfort and style. She got important advice from Jackson Hole resident

Stephen Sullivan, a founder of outdoor apparel companies. He realized she had come up with a needed product and, knowing of her skill as a champion ski racer, sensed her determination to pursue whatever she put her mind to. With help from a family friend she contacted a garment manufacturer in Los Angeles that had good labor practices. Like an experienced entrepreneur, Megan invested her time and savings into a venture that she not only felt passionate about but also sensed would succeed.

Megan's Kickstarter campaign to raise funds far exceeded her $25,000 goal. More than 1,000 donors, many of them young girls and parents, enthusiastically offered financial support. From the design of the Yellowberry bras to the style of promotional photos and the voice of the advertising, Megan's philosophy shone through. "This company is my effort to help other girls who feel the same way I do: that our society pressures us to look and dress a certain way at a very young age. . . . Mary Margaret should feel confident in whatever she wears, not that she is lesser than her peers if she looks different than a goddesslike model 10 years her elder," expressed Megan on her website.

As intended, Megan had created simple, age-appropriate, and comfortable apparel for girls. Her girl-friendly alternative to the supersexualized fashion world that targets adolescent girls attracted the attention of the media. Across the United States and from Australia to the United Kingdom news outlets reported on Yellowberry using phrases like "feminist approach," "training bra for the 21st century," and "bra revolution." The public clearly understood and embraced Megan's mission. She was the right person at the right time to shift the status quo. Her mom, who doubted Megan at first, recalled, "She came to me and said, 'I want to change the bra industry.' I thought: 'Are you crazy? What about the big-box stores, Victoria's Secret and all that?' Everybody's so powerful, and here's this little girl."

During her senior year at high school Megan was not only a champion for little sister Mary Margaret and other girls but a champion skier as well. In March 2014, the Jackson Hole High School ski team won the Wyoming state championship. Megan won first place in two races, skiing faster than any male or female racer. As a student at Middlebury College in Vermont and head of a dynamic new fashion company in partnership with her mother, Megan entered her young-adult years with a sense of purpose and accomplishment.

On the day that Megan committed to creating a new type of bra, she felt what so many girls and parents felt. Megan was fed up with sexualized fashions and fashion ads. Like other activists Megan had been spurred on by a need to make a change in her world.

"I didn't care how many adults chuckled at my idea and brushed me away with the wave of a wrist," wrote Megan on her company's website. "Many of them were very successful entrepreneurs who couldn't see that I had more than just an idea. I was told to have fun and enjoy high school, to stop worrying about changing the bra industry. But I am most inspired and motivated to do something when someone tells me that I can't."

With such a can-do attitude it is no wonder Megan found herself included on *Time* magazine's list of the 25 Most Influential Teens of 2014.

PART I

CLAIMING RIGHTS AND RESPECT

MARGARET SANGER

"Woman Must Not Accept;
She Must Challenge"

"I was resolved to seek out the root of the evil, to do something to change the destiny of mothers whose miseries were as vast as the sky." —*Margaret Sanger*

During the month she spent in prison in 1917, Margaret Sanger refused to see herself as a victim. As always she was an observer, and she wrote about the inequities she witnessed. Unlike male prisoners, female convicts were not allowed to write letters or read newspapers. Many of her fellow female inmates were being jailed indefinitely for minor offenses and were too poor to hire lawyers to challenge their detention. Margaret lost 15 pounds due to being fed a diet of only bread and molasses, with an occasional stew. Though she suffered from fatigue resulting from her chronic tuberculosis, Margaret summoned the energy to counsel the women in prison on sexual matters, as well as to teach illiterate inmates to read and write.

When she was released, 200 friends and supporters greeted her by singing "La Marseillaise," the anthem of American radicals.

―――――

Margaret was born September 14, 1879, in a small run-down cottage on the outskirts of Corning, New York. She was the sixth child of her Irish American parents, Anne and Michael Higgins. Like many other Irish immigrants, both of their families had left Cork, Ireland, during the Great Famine in the late 1840s. So many immigrants from Cork had settled in Corning that one neighborhood was known as Corktown.

Margaret's father supported the family by cutting and adorning headstones. Margaret was raised more by her older sisters than her mother, who was always either pregnant or nursing a baby and constantly fatigued by overwork and illness. At age eight, Margaret (called Maggie by family members) assumed her older sisters' duties as they married and left home. She helped her mother with the care of her younger sister, Ethel, and four younger brothers. Each day she minded a big pot of soup, the family's daily meal, and assisted her mother with the extra laundry they took in to make ends meet.

Her father, Michael Higgins, was a storyteller and rabble-rouser with strong views about the rights of workers and what he saw as the evils of capitalism and the tyranny of the Catholic Church. As a result of his views, one Christmastime when Maggie tried to join some other children at the Parish Hall, a priest turned her away, calling her the "child of the Devil." When Michael invited a popular and controversial orator to speak in Corning, the pastor of the Catholic church convinced officials to lock the doors of the town's only public hall. Undaunted, Michael took Maggie by the hand as he led the audience to a clearing in the woods, where the speech was delivered from a tree stump. Maggie was greatly influenced by the way her father questioned authority and the way he urged her to develop her own ideas.

Maggie's classmates teased her for wearing hand-me-down clothes, but she ignored them. Michael Higgins taught his children to hold their heads high and to consider themselves as people who were special. He encouraged them to take on challenges. Maggie understood this to mean challenges that were physical as well as social. One day she decided to walk across the long railroad bridge spanning the Chemung River. When she was halfway across, a train approached. Maggie stumbled, fell through a gap in the tracks, and hung precariously above the river as the train rumbled overhead. Luckily a passing boatman came to her rescue.

A bright, hardworking student, Maggie was undaunted by having to study in her chaotic and cramped house. Her older sisters paid her tuition to Claverack College, a coeducational boarding school, where Maggie blossomed. She was fascinated with her studies, which varied from drama and art to economics and literature. Maggie became a leader among her classmates, even though most of them came from wealthier families. A keen observer, she learned how to dress, style her hair, dance, and serve tea like her fellow students. Fun loving and full of curiosity, she attracted followers who once joined her in breaking a school rule to traipse off to a dance in the nearby town.

Margaret's wonderful experiences at school abruptly ended when her sisters were no longer able to pay the tuition. Without a college degree Margaret would have to postpone her goal of attending medical school. After an unpleasant year teaching at a school in New Jersey, where she had a class with 84 students, Margaret went home to care for her dying mother in 1899. At 49 years of age, Anne Higgins was succumbing to tuberculosis.

Margaret felt bitter. She felt her mother's 18 pregnancies and 11 childbirths in 22 years, as well as her never-ending chores, had sent her to an early grave. Deciding not to live that kind of life, Margaret left Corning hoping never to return. With the help of one of her Claverack friends she gained admission to the nursing school at White Plains Hospital. Margaret reasoned that with a nursing degree she could support herself, and she could go to medical school after she had saved enough money for tuition.

Margaret excelled at nursing from the start. During her first year she was appointed head nurse of a six-bed ward. Obstetrics became her specialty, and she delivered babies on her own. However, the long hours took their toll. During one three-day period she slept only four hours. She lost weight, looked as pale as her patients, experienced afternoon fevers and night sweats: Margaret had tuberculosis. Her health improved in the spring of 1901 when a physician removed some of her swollen lymph nodes.

At a dance one year later she met handsome William Sanger, a draftsman and artist who was studying to become an architect. Like her father, William denounced capitalism and saw salvation in socialism. Like the Higginses, his parents were immigrants, two of the many Jews who had left Germany, where William was born.

That following summer, in August 1902, William and Margaret married. Because it was forbidden for nursing students to be married, Margaret had to cut her studies short once more. She could not earn certification as a registered nurse, and she left equipped with a diploma as only a practical nurse. By Christmas she was pregnant. Her tuberculosis flared up, and the doctor recommended rest in a cold climate. Margaret started treatment at a sanatorium in Saranac, New York. She slowly improved during her six months there, but she grew bored and returned to the Bronx in time to give birth to their son Stuart in 1903. After Stuart's birth Margaret suffered a relapse and returned to Saranac for another year.

Margaret began a life as mother and wife in a suburb when the family moved north of New York City to Hastings-on-the-Hudson. In 1908 she gave birth to another son, Grant, and two years later a daughter, Peg, was born. Soon after Peg's birth Margaret realized she needed more in life than being a suburban mother and wife. At her insistence they sold their home and in 1910, just before Christmas, moved to New York City. Margaret worked as a visiting nurse in Manhattan's Lower East Side, and

Margaret Sanger with her son Grant.
Courtesy of Library of Congress LC-USZ62-120813

she soon established her own practice in obstetrics, delivering babies and caring for mothers and babies after the birth.

Many of the mothers Margaret treated wanted to know how to prevent further pregnancies. Wishing she knew more, Margaret answered as best as she could. Then one night in the summer of 1912 Margaret was called in to help 28-year-old Sadie Sachs, who had a serious infection after a self-inflicted abortion. After recovery Sadie wanted to know what she could do to prevent another pregnancy. She had three children and didn't want any more. The doctor laughed and told her not to sleep with her husband.

Months later Margaret was called back to the Sachses' apartment. Pregnant again, Sadie had once again tried to abort the baby. This time, despite Margaret's care, she died, leaving behind an anguished husband and three children.

Margaret was distraught. "I resolved that women should have the knowledge of contraception," she later said. "I would tell the world what was going on in the lives of these poor women, I would be heard. No matter what it cost. I would be heard."

Margaret started writing a column, "The Woman's Page," for the *New York Call*, and she gave speeches at open-air meetings. In the Sunday edition she wrote a column called "What Every Mother Should Know" that addressed sex education and what approaches to take with different ages of children. Eventually her discussions of male and female anatomy, birth control, and sexually transmitted diseases prompted the *New York Times* to label her "an enemy of the young."

Margaret and William, known as Bill, now socialized with a crowd in Greenwich Village that included writers, artists, publishers, socialites, and social activists. Bill soon lost interest in this group, but Margaret was thrilled by the fervor and intelligence of her new friends. In turn, her exuberance and passion

BACK-ALLEY TRAGEDIES

In the United States during the late 1800s, abortion, a process by which a pregnancy is terminated, became illegal. Afterward, about one million women per year had either self-induced or "back-alley" abortions. Often performed by unqualified practitioners, many back-alley abortions ended in tragedy, causing either the woman's death or the inability to bear children in the future. In 1973 the US Supreme Court ruled that women have the right to have abortions.

for change attracted attention. Like her father, Margaret enjoyed being listened to and, also like him, she would become a leader. Bill and Margaret drifted apart as she spent more time away from home.

In 1914 Margaret started her own magazine, *The Woman Rebel*, which bore the masthead "No gods. No masters." She intended it to be a rallying cry for women to rise up to demand change. In this forum, she could express her thoughts freely. She published articles about sex education, unequal pay for women, and contraception, using the term *birth control* for the first time in print.

"A woman's body belongs to herself alone. It does not belong to the United States of America or any other nation on earth," Margaret wrote in arguing for contraception. Some people responded to her writings with interest and support, but others responded with disgust. It didn't take long for the US Postal

Service, as enforcer of the Comstock Law, to confiscate copies of *The Woman Rebel*. And not long after, a warrant was served for Margaret's arrest. The charges were serious enough to land her in prison for up to 40 years.

As she awaited trial, Margaret took an even more radical step by publishing the pamphlet *Family Limitation*. Dry as the title may seem today, it was sure to provoke authorities. The pamphlet contained detailed articles on birth control devices, using medical terms such as *penis* and *vagina*. Articles that discussed female sexuality were a direct confrontation with the law. Even though the pamphlet was printed and sold in secret it soon reached the hands of thousands of women desperate for the information and ideas Margaret provided.

COMSTOCK LAW

In 1873 the Comstock Law (named for US Postal Inspector Anthony Comstock) made it illegal to send any materials deemed obscene through the mail. This included any publications mentioning contraception, sexual functions, or homosexuality; photographs of nude or scantily clad women; and actual contraceptives. Over the years there were many court challenges to this act, particularly concerning sex education, birth control information, and contraceptives. In 1972, the US Supreme Court ruled to legalize the mailing of contraceptives and birth control information.

"Jail has not been my goal. There is special work to do and I shall do it first," wrote Margaret to her supporters before fleeing the country for exile in England. Bill joined her for a short period, and the children were at boarding school. When Bill returned to the States, he lived in his art studio. Bill and other supporters secretly dispensed copies of *Family Limitation*. On September 15, 1915, Bill was tried for distributing obscene materials and sentenced to a month in prison. Now both he and Margaret were a cause célèbre.

Margaret returned in mid-October ready to face her trial. A month later their five-year-old daughter, Peg, suddenly died from pneumonia. Bill and Margaret were devastated, as was seven-year-old Grant, who had lost his closest family member. With the trial approaching, Margaret's passion for her cause distracted her from her grief.

The trial was now a political hot potato for the prosecutor and judge. A story of her impending trial with a photograph of Margaret with Stuart and Grant had been published in newspapers across the country. Margaret's demure appearance and her recent loss of a child ensured her the status of a martyr who would gain even more support if convicted of the trumped-up charges. The government dropped the case. Margaret hit the road to drum up more support by giving 119 speeches in cities across the country.

Well aware that public opinion about birth control was shifting, Margaret decided her next step was to open a birth control clinic, defying a New York law that prohibited providing information about birth control. Located in Brooklyn, the clinic opened on October 16, 1916. Staffed by Margaret; her sister, Ethel, now a nurse; and other colleagues, it was the first clinic in the United States dedicated to women's reproductive health.

Women flocked to the new clinic, joined by the press. The police came for Margaret 10 days later. With dramatic flair she refused to ride in the police wagon and marched with a crowd of her supporters to the jail one mile away. After being released on bail to await her trial, Margaret opened a new clinic in a different location, and she was arrested once more. She was sentenced to 30 days in jail, making her a martyr for the cause. Meanwhile her relationship with Bill Sanger came to an end, and Margaret asked for a divorce.

For five years Margaret had been dreaming of a pill that would prevent pregnancy. In 1917 this dream moved closer to a reality. While giving a speech in Boston she met Katharine McCormick, a wealthy biologist and suffragist. Katharine shared Margaret's dreams, and the two women became close friends.

To better educate the public about birth control and to build support for overturning the Comstock Law Margaret started a new journal, the *Birth Control Review*. The front page of the first issue featured an article titled, "Should We Break the Law?" It cited Moses, Christ, Joan of Arc, and abolitionists as examples of lawbreakers who were "beacons of light for human progress."

Four years later, in 1921, Margaret established the American Birth Control League, which would later become the Planned Parenthood Federation.

No longer in a marriage, Margaret was enjoying her freedom. Many men pursued her, but she wasn't persuaded to marry again until she met J. Noah Slee, a 60-year-old divorced man. Noah had made a fortune managing the successful Three-in-One Oil Company, which made a popular lubricant for everything from bicycles to sewing machines to hinges. He was kind to Margaret, attentive to her son Grant, and showered her with gifts. Soon they fell in love and were married on September 18,

1922. The next year Margaret opened the first legal birth control clinic in the country by using a loophole in the law that allowed her to offer contraception for health reasons. Located on Fifth Avenue in New York City, the clinic was staffed by female physicians and social workers.

Margaret fervently sought more followers. In one case, she made a poor choice when she tried to enlist supporters of eugenics. This controversial philosophy advocated for the "improvement" of the genetic makeup of the human race through supporting higher reproduction of classes or cultures its followers deemed as having "good" traits and reducing reproduction of classes or cultures with traits they considered "bad."

Mainstream eugenicists rejected Margaret's ideas, but attempting to associate with them was a dangerous strategy. Like many of them, she supported controlling population growth and reducing the frequency of undesirable genetic attributes, such as hereditary diseases. Unlike them, however, Margaret did not support the idea of decreasing populations of certain ethnic groups such as Jews or African Americans. Unfortunately, not all her writings on the subject were clearly thought out, and some of her allies lost respect for her. Some of her statements provided fodder to anti–birth control adversaries who sought to destroy her reputation.

From the 1920s through the late 1930s Margaret wrote five books with combined sales of almost one million copies. In 1951 she had a chance meeting with biologist and researcher Dr. Gregory Pincus, who took an interest in hormonal contraceptive research. Margaret encouraged his research, and Katharine McCormick enthusiastically provided funds for Pincus and his colleagues. Less than 10 years later, in 1960, the US Food and Drug Administration approved "the pill" for use. Margaret Sanger had lived long enough to see her wish come true.

Margaret passed away at her home in Tucson, Arizona, on September 6, 1966. This daughter of poor Irish immigrants had been a firebrand, taking on the mantle of the birth control movement. Almost 50 years after her death Margaret continues to be viewed both as a hero and a demon. As with all people there are many sides to her story, but what stands out is her courage to advocate for the rights of others.

ALICE PAUL

Equal Rights for Women

"I have never doubted that equal rights was the right direction. Most reforms, most problems are complicated. But to me there is nothing complicated about equal rights." —Alice Paul

---

On the morning of November 9, 1909, London bobbies were on the lookout for militant suffragettes who might cause a disruption at the lord mayor's banquet scheduled for that evening. Disguised as charwomen, Alice Paul and Amelia Brown entered Guildhall and hid on the balcony that overlooked the hall where guests would dine. That evening another one of their team, Lucy Burns, masquerading as a guest, gained admission to the hall. As cabinet member Winston Churchill and his wife arrived, Lucy waved a small flag in his face as she asked, "How can you dine here while women are starving in prison?" It was a reference to imprisoned suffragettes. Police immediately dragged her out of the hall.

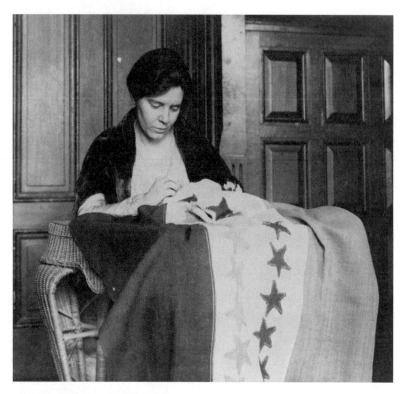

Alice Paul sewing a suffrage flag.
Courtesy of Library of Congress LC-USZ62-119710

Meanwhile Amelia and Alice waited for their act of civil dis-
obedience. Just as Prime Minister Herbert Henry Asquith began
his speech, Amelia smashed a window with her shoe and then
both she and Alice shouted, "Votes for women!" Police arrested
them and a judge sentenced them to a month of hard labor in
prison. Before Alice came to England, she had never broken the
law or made a scene. Alice's mother couldn't understand what
had happened to her "mild-mannered girl."

Alice Stokes Paul was born on January 11, 1885, to devout Quakers William and Tacie Paul, who lived in the Quaker community of Moorestown, New Jersey. Eight generations before, in 1685, her ancestor Phillip Paul had fled England in pursuit of religious freedom. The Pauls lived on their 167-acre farm surrounded by other Quakers who valued learning and tranquility. The family income from William's job as a bank president, as well as the earnings from the farm, ensured a comfortable life. As was customary, Quaker neighbors and family wore plain clothes and used *thee* and *thou* in their daily speech. Most girls traveled to school in carriages, but Alice preferred riding bareback on her horse. She loved reading, and over the years she read every book in both her family and school libraries.

Quakers, also known as Friends, had strong moral convictions. They were opposed to both war and slavery. Tacie Paul's grandparents, as followers of Quaker leader Elias Hicks, opposed slavery by boycotting any products such as cane sugar, cotton, or other goods produced using slave labor. Many men in Moorestown had been imprisoned for refusing to serve as soldiers or to pay taxes for the military.

Lucretia Mott, a Quaker minister, suffragist, and abolitionist, had been a visitor to the home of Alice's great-grandparents. In 1848 Mott had helped organize the first convention devoted to winning women the right to vote. Despite nearly 50 years of striving for the right, suffragists had still not achieved it by the time Alice reached womanhood.

Alice's mother, Tacie, was one of the first female students at Swarthmore. This coed college had been founded by followers of Hicks, including Tacie's father, to provide equal educational opportunities for women. In 1901, at the age of 16, Alice moved to Swarthmore, elated with her newfound freedom. That spring, her father died from pneumonia. He had been a busy, remote, and strict husband and father. He believed that each day should be devoted to work or silence and that music might be harmful. Rather than casting a pall over the household, his passing let some light in. Tacie bought a piano and permitted her younger daughter, Helen, to take lessons.

Just before graduation, one of Alice's professors suggested that she pursue a career in social work. After she finished school, she left for New York City and lived for the first time outside the bubble of Quaker tranquility. Her lodging was in the College Settlement located in the heart of Manhattan's melting pot, the Lower East Side. It was an eye-opening experience, but after a year Alice decided that social work was not for her. Instead she chose to study sociology and earned a master's degree at the University of Pennsylvania. Her academic accomplishments prompted her community in Moorestown to award her a scholarship at Woodbroke, a Friends' study center on an estate in Birmingham, England, donated by Quaker candy maker George Cadbury.

Alice found her path and passion at Woodbroke. In December 1907 Alice listened in fascination as Christabel Pankhurst delivered a powerful speech demanding the right to vote for women. Beautiful and eloquent, Christabel, who had just earned her law degree, captivated the audience. Afterward Alice felt her "heart and soul convert" to the cause. Soon she would be caught up in the fervor of the Pankhurst family. In 1870, Christabel's father, Richard, had written the first bill introduced to Parliament to give women the vote. Following his death, Christabel's mother, Emmeline, established the Women's Social and Political Union (WSPU) to carry on the cause.

Alice was struggling to make ends meet, despite earning money for her work at a settlement house (see page 113) and receiving money from home. She wondered if she should just

WOMEN'S SOCIAL AND POLITICAL UNION

Using the motto Deeds Not Words, the Women's Social and Political Union split from more moderate suffragists to increase the pressure on the English government to award women the right to vote. Using more confrontational tactics to gain publicity, they soon gained a reputation as militants. In reaction to imprisonment of members for destruction of property and disruption of government proceedings, WSPU prisoners started hunger strikes.

pack up and head back to New Jersey as her mother suggested. Alice had lost interest in working at settlement houses. As a graduate of Swarthmore, she could apply for a scholarship to study abroad. When the scholarship was denied, Alice was uncertain what to do next. When she received an invitation from her hero, Emmeline Pankhurst, to participate in more daring and dangerous activities, Alice accepted.

She had endured men's crude, lewd jeers when selling WSPU newspapers and giving street-corner speeches. Now, as she took this next assignment, she understood that imprisonment was a definite possibility. Though worried about disgracing her family and friends, the stories she had heard about her Quaker ancestors who were imprisoned for their principles gave her the courage to take the leap. On her first mission, on June 29, 1909, she marched along with other WSPU militants to Parliament to demand a meeting with the prime minister. Upon reaching the entrance guarded by 3,000 officers, Emmeline Pankhurst was informed that a meeting was not possible. In response she gently slapped a policeman so that she and other elderly women leaders would be arrested and taken away. This was a signal for the younger women to charge into the police lines.

"The police grabbed the suffragettes by the throats & threw themselves on their backs over & over again. The mounted police rode us down again & again," wrote Alice in a letter to her mother. This was the first of many times Alice would be arrested. It was also her first meeting, at the police station, with another American prisoner with bright red hair and a charming smile by the name of Lucy Burns. The two had much in common and would become compatriots.

Charges were dropped for this first arrest, but after her next arrest Alice was sent to the notorious Holloway women's prison. Like other militants, she went on hunger strike for being denied status as a political prisoner. She was soon too weak to walk and was released more than a week early from her two-week sentence. The hunger strikes served as a successful publicity ploy to highlight the government's brutality against suffragists. Charges were dropped after Alice's next arrest in Norwich, and she and Lucy Burns left for Scotland soon after to help Emmeline prepare for a big rally in the coming fall.

The authorities were not so lenient after the episode at Guildhall in November 1909; they initiated a new policy to force-feed hunger strikers like Alice by inserting a five-foot-long tube through her nose. This cruel and extremely painful procedure was tantamount to torture. Her arrest made news in American newspapers, but the unsympathetic reporters misreported her actions and defamed her character. Nonetheless, Alice became a hero to suffragists around the world. After a month in prison, Alice told her mother she was coming home and explained that her compatriots' decision to "resist prison" through hunger strikes was "simply a policy of passive resistance" that Quakers should approve of.

Alice carried home with her a reputation as one of the new generation of suffragists. She was on the roster of speakers at the National Woman Suffrage Association (NWSA or National) convention in April 1910. There she met prominent NWSA leaders such as Anna Howard Shaw, who was almost 40 years her senior. In the 41 years since the NWSA's founding, despite the hard work of suffragists Susan B. Anthony and Elizabeth Cady Stanton, a suffrage bill had only been voted on once in Congress, in 1887. Since then they had tried to win the right to vote on a state-by-state basis, but progress was painfully slow. Younger women like Alice and Lucy were full of energy and impatient for progress.

For the next three years Alice threw herself into the suffrage campaign as she worked hard earning a doctorate in economics from the University of Pennsylvania. Her major professor commented on the "brilliance of her mind" and her devotion "to lifting the low condition of women." Alice now knew that her future was not in academia but in the passion that Christabel had stirred years before. Turning down offers to work for several state suffrage organizations, she quietly asked for and was awarded the chairwomanship of NWSA's congressional committee in the nation's capital. With the help of Lucy Burns, as vice-chair, Alice then proceeded to build the committee into a potent political force.

Their first major task was to organize a grand suffrage parade during the same week as President Wilson's inauguration. Meant to bring attention to the suffragists' cause, it did so in an unintended way. As they paraded on March 3, 1912, male hooligans verbally and physically attacked women while police stood by offering the women no protection. The attack on the parade made national headlines as newspapers condemned both the attackers and police, winning sympathy for the suffragists.

Without a pause Alice and her team tirelessly drummed up new members, funds, and support for a national suffrage bill. Alice was only 28 years old in March 1913 when she had her first meeting with President Woodrow Wilson. She was hoping he would lend his support for suffrage, but he blithely stated he had no opinion on the matter. On subsequent visits, he continued to stonewall the suffragists, so Alice turned her focus to Congress. In April the federal suffrage amendment was introduced in both the House and Senate. On July 31, 1913, Alice led a procession of 500 women in merrily festooned automobiles to the Capitol where they delivered petitions with 80,000 signatures and then listened to the first Senate debate on suffrage in 26 years. The result was positive as 21 senators voted in favor of the amendment.

As Alice and her team moved ahead with new work, tensions grew between her congressional committee and NWSA headquarters. Meanwhile on the other side of the Atlantic, Alice's hero Emmeline Pankhurst called for "guerilla warfare" to overcome Parliament's refusal to even consider granting women the vote. Announcing, "no votes, no golf," suffragists damaged golf courses, the playgrounds of rich and powerful men. When Pankhurst, whom the NWSA leadership denounced, came to the United States to raise funds, Alice enthusiastically assisted her. Feeling restrained by the NWSA leadership, in 1916 Alice and her supporters established the National Woman's Party (NWP).

Progress toward getting another vote for the suffrage amendment stalled. A favorite saying of Tacie Paul's was, "When you put your hand to the plow, you can't put it down until you get to the end of the row." Alice took these words to heart as she led the slow, steady march to victory. President Wilson was not budging so Alice and her team decided to stage the first-ever picketing demonstration at the White House gates. Known as the Silent Sentinels, the picketers displayed banners with messages such as "What will you do, Mr. President, for half the people of this nation?"

On April 6, 1917, the United States entered World War I. As war dominated the news the banner messages became more inflammatory. On June 20 the banner read, "We the women of America, tell you that America is not a democracy. Twenty million women are denied the right to vote. President Wilson is the chief opponent of their national enfranchisement."

In the pro-war fervor, freedom of speech was becoming a thing of the past. An angry crowd tore the banner from the women's hands. Newspapers supported the mob violence, calling the wording treasonous. When the chief of police for the District of Columbia ordered Alice to end the picketing she boldly refused. The next group of picketing suffragists was immediately arrested. Since the women weren't breaking any law, the police charged them with obstructing traffic and then released them without penalties. As they continued to picket, the repression increased. They were charged with violating the District's Peace and Order Act, a vague law that encompassed numerous offenses. The first group of picketers charged under this act received a three-day sentence. The next group, who displayed a banner that got no one upset, was shocked after being sentenced to 60 days in a workhouse notorious for its cruel warden.

The judge was following a new agenda that permitted harsh punishment as a means to silence dissent. The women's supporters protested loudly, but their leader was silent. Alice was severely ill in a clinic—she was diagnosed with Bright's disease, a kidney disease, and given a prognosis of only one more year to live. President Wilson yielded to the protest and pardoned the women after three days.

In August picketers marched to the White House gates with Alice in the lead. An awaiting mob seized the banner and knocked the women, including Alice, to the ground. Alice was sentenced to seven months in the crowded and filthy District jail. When she went on hunger strike to protest denial of status as a political prisoner, she was force-fed. When supporters stood outside the jail to cheer her on, she was moved to a window-less room in the psychiatric ward on the pretext that she was insane. Dozens of other suffragists were also jailed, many who also went on hunger strikes and were force-fed. When reports of their mistreatment leaked out, the public outcry that resulted led to an early release for Alice. Perhaps sensing this shift in public opinion, on January 10, 1918, President Wilson finally pledged support of the suffrage amendment.

Now Alice and the party stalwarts worked around the clock lobbying legislators in both the House and the Senate. Using all their contacts, they won over lawmakers one by one. Finally the amendment passed the House on May 21, 1919, and then the Senate less than two weeks later on June 4. Now the National Woman's Party took on the task of making sure the legislatures of 36 states ratified the amendment so it could become part of the US Constitution. Just like the nail-biting finale of a sports event, by the summer of 1920 the ratification of only one more state was needed. At the last minute a legislator from Tennes-see switched his vote at the urging of his mother, making the amendment the law.

For the women of the United States it had been a long, long journey. Women such as Lucretia Mott, Susan B. Anthony, Elizabeth Cady Stanton, Anna Howard Shaw, Carrie Chapman Catt, and finally the young "militant" suffragists such as Alice

Paul and Lucy Burns, had kept the fight alive for more than 70 years. Some were ready to rest and move on to other things, but Alice had one more goal. Having the right to vote didn't guarantee women other rights or equality in legal issues such as child custody, property rights, and numerous other civil rights. An equal rights amendment was needed.

Alice wrote the first draft of the Equal Rights Amendment (ERA) in 1923 while she was earning two law degrees. Each year the amendment was brought before Congress for a vote and failed to gain passage until 1972. At 87 years old Alice Paul celebrated its passage by both houses of Congress, but by the time of her death on July 9, 1977, it hadn't been ratified. In fact, the ERA has *still* not been ratified. Perhaps 100 years after women won the vote a new generation of women will make Alice's dream come true.

MAGGIE KUHN

◆

Young and Old Together

"Old age is an excellent time for outrage. My goal is to say or do at least one outrageous thing a week." —*Maggie Kuhn*

Maggie Kuhn received an invitation to the White House to watch President Gerald Ford sign a bill that would regulate private pensions, which are retirement funds provided by companies. Maggie accepted the honor, but she didn't come to the White House to celebrate. She didn't think the bill was sufficient to solve many of the problems facing retirees, and she hoped for a chance to speak to the president about those concerns. She was seated with others around a large table in the Cabinet Room. After the bill signing everyone tried to get Ford's attention. Maggie's waving hand was lost in the sea of higher hands, but finally he noticed her.

"Young lady, do you have something to say?" he asked.

Sixty-nine-year-old Maggie had a great sense of humor, but she didn't think this question was cute or funny. Instead of

26

Maggie Kuhn in the 1970s.
Courtesy of Julie Jensen

starting her carefully prepared statement, she spoke
her mind, "Mr. President, I
am not a young lady, I am an
old woman." What followed
was a moment of uncom-
fortable silence while the
flustered president regained
his composure.

Maggie Kuhn was born in Buffalo, New York, on August 3,
1905, in the house of her Dutch grandmother. This home on
Eagle Street was ruled by two generations of strongly independent widows. Maggie's mother, Minnie, and her aunt Paulina
had grown up there and helped their mother, Maggie's grandmother Kooman, run the family store. After attending business
school Minnie managed the store's accounts.

Maggie's father, Samuel, was the oldest of 10 children. As a
boy, he was forced to drop out of school to help support his family and, by the time he married Minnie, he was working with a
credit company. Two years before Maggie's birth, he was transferred to Memphis, Tennessee.

It was a hard move for Minnie. She was appalled by the racism of her white neighbors, who shunned her for regarding her black maid as an equal. When it came time for Minnie to give birth to Maggie, she returned to Buffalo to be with her family, as she would again three years later to give birth to Maggie's brother, Sam, a frail, sickly child. He would always need special care, and he was later diagnosed with mental illness.

Maggie was five when her father was transferred to Louisville, Kentucky. Returning north to Buffalo for part of the summer to spend time with extended family became a yearly event. Maggie felt especially close to spirited Aunt Paulina. In later years Maggie discovered that Paulina had marched with other suffragists demanding the right to vote—and that one time she took off her hat at a rally, at that time a rebellious act for a proper woman. Aunt Paulina became Maggie's model of womanhood.

When Maggie was 10, her father was once again transferred, this time to Cleveland, Ohio. Maggie graduated from high school there at age 16. She hoped to go east to attend Vassar or Wellesley College, but her father insisted that she study in Cleveland at the College for Women at Western Reserve University. In the 1920s only 1 out of 12 American women went to college. Maggie knew this was a great opportunity, as was getting permission to live on campus. As part of her sociology class she went on field trips to a jail, social welfare institutions, sweatshops, and slums rife with rat-infested houses. This was Maggie's first glimpse into the other side of Cleveland. She felt compassion for the people living there. When she told her father that the poor were underpaid, ignored, and abused, he became furious. He hadn't needed help, he said, why should anyone else?

Maggie would also find out how uncompromising her father was when she started dating young men. Maggie had a pas-

YWCA

In 1855, Lady Mary Jane Kinnaird and Christian Emma Robarts started the Young Women's Christian Association to support single young women in London. The YWCA provided housing and activities to build mind, body, and spirit. In 1866 the first American YWCA opened in Boston. The "Y" became known for its pools and gyms, but it also provided employment bureaus, health clinics, and aid to single women travelers. It supported the rights of workers to unionize, encouraged members to take a stand against lynchings, and made birth control services more accessible. In 2013 more than two million people benefited from YWCA services.

sionate romance with the son of the church pastor; her father thought the young man lacked ambition. She refused her beau's marriage proposal, as she would future offers.

Following college Maggie began working at the YWCA, teaching working women a wide range of subjects such as unionizing and consumer advocacy. Because she was still living at home, Maggie joined her family when they moved to Philadelphia in 1930, and she transferred to the local YWCA. Her most popular class there was about marriage and human sexuality. During this era young women received no sex education, so for many of her students it was the first time they had ever talked about their bodies. The course covered everything from the mechanics of sexual intercourse to birth control, sexual pleasure, pregnancy, motherhood, and the challenge of being single in a culture where marriage was the norm. Working for the YWCA, Maggie was surrounded by dynamic and dedicated women coworkers and administrators. Most of them were single, and that looked good to Maggie, who envisioned a life with more freedom than she felt a wife had. Later when asked why she never married, Maggie would reply, "Sheer luck."

When the United States entered World War II Maggie moved to New York City and lived on her own for the first time. While the men were off fighting, women were recruited to replace them as workers at factories producing aircraft, weapons, and ammunition. Maggie helped the women workers adjust to their new lives. She found housing and childcare for them, and she set up social activities and classes they could attend after work.

In 1950, at the age of 45, Maggie returned to Philadelphia to help care for her aging parents. She took a new, better-paying job at the headquarters of the Presbyterian Church. Before the church leaders would take a position on social issues, such as racial segregation or violations of civil rights, they required background information to support their decision. It was Maggie's task to assemble the facts and figures needed to back up the church's stance on each particular issue. Before long she had a reputation for being a thorough researcher. She learned how to argue for a cause and that if you speak out you had better do your homework first.

After Maggie's father, Samuel, passed away in 1955, she bought a large stone house in Germantown, an old section of Philadelphia. She moved in with her brother, Sam, and their mother, who died just six months later. Maggie's insights into the problems of elders gained from caring for her parents helped at work, where she was now investigating issues facing elders.

She was disturbed to see old people in retirement homes being treated like children. She observed that many retirement home residents were willing and able to help manage the facilities they lived in. She convinced the church to include elderly residents in the management of church retirement homes.

As the 1960s came to an end, Maggie was still full of energy and ideas as she approached age 65. She was not ready to retire, but like other older workers she would be "put out to pasture" by her employer. In later years her forced retirement would be called "the most significant retirement in modern American history." As the shock wore off, Maggie talked to friends in the same situation, and they came up with a plan to use their skills and wisdom to change the world. Their first mission was to stop the Vietnam War.

"We felt at one with the young war protesters and were disturbed that more of our generation were not speaking out," wrote Maggie.

At first, for lack of a better name, they called themselves the Consultation of Older Persons. Their motto was, "Age and youth in action." They stood shoulder-to-shoulder with students, arguing that the nation should support the needs of the poor, youth, and elders rather than spend millions on war. Despite not having any children of her own, Maggie had informally adopted grandchildren. Two college students moved into her house to help care for her mentally ill brother in exchange for rent. When Maggie was their age, the act of a woman removing her hat in public was defiant; now, in her old age, young women were burning bras at women's liberation rallies.

Maggie teamed up with activist Hobart Jackson after meeting him at a conference on aging. He had transformed a badly managed nursing home for low-income black people into a model facility. Elder care for African Americans, Latinos, and

other minorities was not on the list of topics for the upcoming
White House Conference on Aging. Hobart and Maggie organized the Black House Conference on Aging in Washington,
DC, two weeks before the official conference. It caught the
attention of White House staff, earning Maggie and Hobart
invitations to meet with the conference chairman.

To ensure they would be listened to seriously at the meeting,
Maggie and 75 elders, mostly women, marched to the White
House to demand equal care for all elders regardless of race,
culture, or income, as well as an end to the war. When police
appeared on horses, Maggie doubted they would attack a group
of harmless old people, but they did. One of her friends was
knocked down and hauled off to jail. The White House staff
took notice once more and added the protesters' demands to the
conference agenda.

When Maggie told a television producer about the White
House protest he suggested they rename their group the Gray
Panthers. Maggie doubled over in laughter. This play on the
name of a group of militant black activists, the Black Panthers,
was perfect. It contradicted the notion that old people were
pushovers. "Our new name gave us a sense of urgency, and after
all, we did want to create a stir," wrote Maggie.

The name itself created a buzz and put the Gray Panthers
in the spotlight. The media loved the Gray Panthers' combination of theatrical flair and witty slogans. Consumer advocate
Ralph Nader, who appreciated both the publicity stunts and the
Gray Panthers' careful research, offered his help. Throughout
the country urban elders were being mugged after cashing their
monthly social security checks. For most older people, a checking account was not affordable. The Gray Panthers asked Philadelphia's largest bank to offer elders free checking accounts,
money orders, and loans for those that owned homes, but the

bank president rejected the idea. After the mugging death of an old woman, Maggie asked Ralph Nader for help. By coincidence he knew the bank chairman, who liked the idea and figured out an inexpensive way to provide the service. This triumph for the Gray Panthers was also good publicity for the bank. "Go to the top—that's my advice to anyone who wants to change the system," wrote Maggie.

Elderly people were used to feeling invisible, unneeded, and voiceless. Maggie took on the job of chief myth buster, saying, "Old age is not a disease." Nor were elderly people mindless, sexless, useless, or powerless. The Gray Panthers were disgusted with television's portrayal of old people as bumbling, old-fashioned dimwits. Elders rarely appeared in commercials promoting products other than denture adhesives, vitamins, or laxatives. Why was this? Old people bought cars, cereal, and other products hawked on TV. Maggie and Lydia Bragger, a public relations expert, wrote to the president of CBS about the "pervasive put-downs of the old on TV." Their activism led to a shift in programming.

Besides defending their rights, Maggie also encouraged fellow elders to help "heal and humanize our society" by taking on new roles. Elders could be watchdogs that howl when institutions endanger the public. They could blow the whistle on government and corporate fraud and corruption. Most important, they could educate and mentor youth.

In retirement, Maggie was having more fun than ever before. She could be as bold and brassy as she wanted. Her clever one-liners caught the public's attention: "Don't agonize, organize," "Sex and learning end only when rigor mortis sets in," "Well-aimed slingshots can topple giants."

Maggie was asked to appear on television programs from the *Tonight* show to *Saturday Night Live*. She wrote an autobiography,

No Stone Unturned: The Life and Times of Maggie Kuhn. In 1976 she was asked to run as the vice presidential candidate for the People's Party but declined the honor. She was the subject of an award-winning documentary, *Maggie Growls,* which called her "amazing, canny, lusty, charming, and unstoppable" and claimed she had "fueled a political chain reaction that changed the lives of older Americans, repealing mandatory retirement laws and proving that 'old' is not a dirty word."

Maggie lived freely, making her own rules for relationships, choosing love affairs rather than marriage, and selecting wit as her weapon of choice. To the young people who revered her for mobilizing elders to oppose the Vietnam War, she in turn asked for their support, saying, "Every one of us is growing old."

On April 22, 1995, just months shy of her 90th birthday, Maggie passed away at home surrounded by her family of friends. Twenty years later the Gray Panthers are alive and well, carrying on Maggie's mission to fight "truth decay" and foster age and youth in action.

SAMPAT PAL DEVI

———◆———

Founding the Gulabi Gang

"Village society in India is loaded against women. It refuses to educate them, marries them off too early, barters them for money. Village women need to study and become independent to sort it out themselves." —Sampat Pal Devi

---

The people in one small village in India had one big problem. Without regard for the law, a wealthy landowner had completely blocked a road with a wall as he began construction of a new house, forcing the villagers living on one side of the wall to walk all the way around the village just to get to the other side. The villagers knew from experience that neither the police nor the mayor would help them, so they went to Sampat Pal Devi for help.

Sampat knew how to fix problems. She visited the village mayor to discuss the issue and heard a familiar story: nothing could be done because the police were afraid of the powerful landowner. So Sampat guided the village women in demolishing

Sampat Pal Devi with the Gulabi Gang.
Courtesy of Amana Fontanella-Khan

the wall with picks and hammers. In response, the landowner commanded the police to arrest the mayor's husband. Now it was time to make the police listen to the people.

Sampat led a large mob of women to the police station, where they promptly sat down in the street. When a police official told them they couldn't sit there, Sampat replied that they would stay as long as it took to have the mayor's husband released. Her tactic worked and soon he was free, but Sampat wasn't done. She led the women to the local judge to file a complaint against the police official that had served the landlord and not the people. Faced with a crowd of women outside his office, the judge accepted their demand to fire the officer. Sampat knew that a crowd of resolute women is a powerful force.

Sampat Pal Devi was born in 1958 in the small village of Kairi, in the region of Bundelkhand in central India. Her father, Ramasrey, whom she called Bappu, worked such long hours herding cows and goats and tending his crops that she barely saw him. Her mother, Gudia, whom she called Amma, went silently about her tasks at home and in the fields. Both were illiterate and, like other members of their family, belonged to the Gadaria caste. Living with them was her grandmother Dai, who showered Sampat with love. Also sharing the home was her father's educated younger brother, Chunni Lal, and his wife. He would carry Sampat on his shoulders for hours and loved to make her smile. "I was a happy girl who never had to do any chores. In fact I was free to do as I pleased," remembered Sampat.

Sampat grew into a willful, adventurous, and sometimes irresponsible child. One day when she was tasked with guarding the family's newly planted rice seedlings from hungry water buffalo, she decided to abandon her post to follow some boys on their way to school. Squatting at the edge of the open-air classroom, Sampat watched in fascination as the teacher instructed students in writing the Hindi alphabet. As they used chalk to copy each letter on slate boards she scratched out each letter in the dust.

From that day on Sampat left the field to listen to the lessons. Within a week she had learned the whole alphabet. Then one day as she was intently writing letters in the dust, she had the shock of looking up to see her uncle's angry face. He was ready to scold her for letting the buffalo eat the seedlings, but his anger turned to joy when he realized she had taken her education into her own hands. He convinced Bappu and Amma to send her to school, where she learned so quickly that she skipped grades.

Sampat's education in Kairi came to an end when her father bought farmland 30 miles away near the tiny village of Hanuman Dhara. Situated atop a small hill on the edge of the jungle,

CASTE SYSTEM

Known as *jati*, the caste system in India is an ancient Hindu social structure that divides people into four main groups called *varnas*, the Sanskrit word meaning colors. At the top of the hierarchy are the Brahmins, or learned class, followed by the Kshatriyas, associated with rulers, warriors, and property owners, and then the Vaishyas, comprising businesspeople. The final caste, the Shudras, is made up of the workers. Each *varna* includes subgroups, such as the herders—Gadaria—Sampat's family's caste. Outside of this traditional order was a fifth group considered too low to be included, known as Dalits, or untouchables. Due to their professions as leatherworkers, garbage haulers, or toilet cleaners they were considered too impure for the other varnas to associate with. They were denied educations or the opportunity to change professions. Though caste-based discrimination and enforcing "untouchability" was outlawed in 1950, both are still common in India.

this village was too small to have a school. Sampat roamed the fields with other girls and learned to climb trees as fast as a monkey. Amma was not happy with her daughter's antics, but Grandmother Dai defended Sampat saying, "Stop bothering your daughter. You can see you are no match for her."

Sampat was already straining against the chains that bound women in her culture. She wanted to speak her mind, fight back if anyone hit her, and battle injustices. In her rural community, homes lacked outhouses so people relieved themselves in the fields. She and her fellow children used a field that bordered another small community. It was considered neutral territory. One day a gang of girls from the other community said the field was off limits, so Sampat rallied her friends. Defiantly they squatted in full view of their rivals. A battle ensued, in which Sampat outfought the gang's leader. To appease the other adults, Uncle Chunni Lal scolded her in public, but he later told Sampat, "Never let anyone hurt you. If someone attacks you, pay them back in kind."

As was the custom, when Sampat was only 12 years old her parents promised her in marriage to a man from another Gadaria family. Ten years her senior, Munni Lal Pal had been married before, to Sampat's distant cousin who died a short time later. As agreed upon, Sampat moved in with Munni's family in the nearby village of Rauli when she turned 14. She bore her first child, a daughter named Prabhawti, at the age of 15.

In Rauli, the Brahmins were accustomed to taking whatever they wished from people in the lower castes, such as the Gadaria. Sampat's refusal one day to "lend" a Brahmin some sleeping mats, knowing she would never get them back, caused the Brahmin man to yell and scream. It was unheard of for a person of lower caste to deny requests of someone in a higher caste, but Sampat thought her dignity was more important than outlawed customs. Known as the daughter-in-law who was a troublemaker, she made even more waves after exposing the crooked dealings of a village shopkeeper. Her mother-in-law, who cared more about propriety than justice, soon tried to banish Sampat and Munni Lal Pal without a single possession.

Though far younger than her husband, Sampat was made of tougher stuff. Facing the loss of all they owned, she skillfully argued their case before the villagers, and her husband was awarded a portion of the family fields, as well as a woodshed they could use as a house. From this time on, Sampat took her family's destiny into her own hands. She bought a sewing machine with money she had saved, and she sewed clothes to sell in the village. After giving birth to her second daughter, Ambrawati, she set up a small shop in front of their modest home. When village girls came to her eager to learn how to sew, she opened a sewing school. Now she was earning more money than Munni Lal.

One day she was told about a gathering of women in Chitrakoot, a town not far from her parents' home. Certain Munni Lal would not allow her to attend, she falsely told him she needed to visit the doctor. At the meeting Sampat listened to a well-dressed, elegant woman argue for women's rights. These words set her head spinning. "Suddenly the world seemed full of promise and I was beginning to get a vague idea of the role I might play in it."

Munni Lal was furious when he accidently discovered that Sampat had lied to him in order to attend the meeting. Sampat forcefully and successfully explained to him that her desire to educate herself was not a threat to his role as husband. Now with his support, she was free not only to run her sewing school but also to set up women's groups in the region to advocate for women's rights. Sampat continued to protest the restrictions of caste culture, making friends with the Dalits, or untouchables. After she ate food prepared by a Dalit family, her fellow Gadaria refused to let her sit with them. She made enemies in the village in her own and higher castes. When she was 30, she discovered that assassins had been hired to kill her. Fearing the hired killers, Sampat decided to leave. Her two oldest daughters were married, but she still had three children at home. She arrived with her children and Munni Lal in the nearby town of Badusa, where her friend Indrani, a widow, offered them a room. Within months Sampat was back on her feet. This time she established a sewing school for the wives of local policemen, and she set Munni Lal up as a vegetable vendor.

The sewing school was a success and allowed Sampat to begin organizing women to stand up for their rights and to gain economic independence. She helped women to pool their money together so they could offer loans to those wanting to start a small business. In return, those borrowing funds would pay back the money with interest to replenish and increase the group's bank account.

One day Jay Prakash, a social worker doing similar work for an NGO (nongovernmental organization), asked Sampat if she would work with him. She agreed, thinking she had more to gain than lose. The Indian government would pay them for successfully setting up accounts for self-help groups. Together she and Jay, whom she nicknamed Babuji, organized group after group. When they requested the payments they were owed for their work, the government official in charge demanded they give a portion of the money to him. When Sampat and Babuji refused, the official sent some local thugs to threaten them. When they told a policeman of this criminal activity and described the thugs, he refused to help. Instead, he ordered another policeman to arrest Babuji. In a rage Sampat slapped the policeman and then left with Babuji to visit the top police official in the district capital to lodge a complaint about corruption.

As they continued to organize women, Sampat and Babuji came up against one corrupt official after another. Sampat was incensed that these men would refuse to help poor, needy women and would instead defend rich merchants and landlords. Following her successful group action against the landlord who had built his home in the street, Sampat formally organized the Gulabi Gang in 2006.

"Gulabi" is the Hindi word for pink. Pink saris became the uniform of the women's gang, which, at a moment's notice, would rise up to defend victims of violence and corruption. As a Gadaria, Sampat carried a shepherd's staff called a *lathi*. Each gang member learned to use a *lathi* for self-defense and carried it during each action. Together Sampat and her gang punished abusive husbands, forced the police to arrest corrupt merchants, and exposed government officials stealing food rations meant for the poor. They forced police to register and file rape cases. They helped elderly widows obtain government benefits, demanded education for women, and fought to end child marriages and the dowry system.

This idea of women taking initiative to fix a broken system appealed to women throughout the region. Sampat said, "We are not a gang in the usual sense of the term. We are a gang for justice." By 2008, 20,000 women had joined chapters of the Gulabi Gang throughout India and elsewhere. In 2008 Sampat told her life story in the book *Sampat Pal: Warrior in a Pink Sari*. Two years later the release of a documentary about the Gulabi Gang titled *Pink Saris* brought the gang's story to theaters. Later Sampat protested the filming of *Gulaab Gang*, a Bollywood movie loosely based on her life, because the producers had not sought her permission.

Oppressed rural people were rallied into action by Sampat Pal Devi's forceful personality, unwavering convictions, and fearlessness. In turn, with mobs of women standing at her back, Sampat was able to place corrupt and incompetent officials in the spotlight. Like most leaders, however, Sampat had flaws.

She could be authoritative with fellow gang members and made decisions without consulting coworkers, like Babuji. In March 2014 the gang's working committee asked Sampat to step down from her leadership post in the Gulabi Gang. Defiantly, Sampat claimed she still had the support of the majority of gang members. "I have been a fighter," said Sampat in response to her ouster, "and will overcome this tide as well." Meanwhile, the work of the Gulabi Gang she founded continues.

DANA EDELL

---◆---

Girl Power

"How we are represented and who represents us plays a crucial role. Who is telling our stories? Are we speaking for ourselves, or are we being directed by others?" —*Dana Edell*

Carina Cruz, age 16, and Emma Stydahar, age 17, were fed up with digitally manipulated photos of models in magazines such as *Teen Vogue*. In July 2012 the two SPARK bloggers started collecting signatures for a petition titled, "Teen Vogue: Give Us Images of Real Girls." They wrote, "These photoshopped images are extremely dangerous to girls like us who read [teen magazines], because they keep telling us: you are not skinny enough, pretty enough or perfect enough. As teen girls, we know first hand how hurtful the photoshopped pictures in these magazines can be for our body image and self-esteem." Coaching Carina and Emma with the logistics of the campaign was SPARK's director, Dana Edell.

Dana Edell.
Courtesy of Dana Edell

After thousands signed the petition, Emma had the opportunity to promote their cause on a Fox television show. When Dana met up with her early in the morning at Fox studios, she was shocked to see how Emma was dressed. In high heels and a strapless minidress, Emma was indeed striking, but Dana feared that the outfit was inconsistent with the girls' campaign against the media's portrayal of women as sex objects. As a mentor of young women Dana believed that girls should wear whatever they wish, but she was also aware of the hazards of leaving oneself open to attack by opponents.

After telling Emma of her concern they came up with a quick fix. They draped Dana's cardigan over Emma's bare shoulders. With a sigh of relief Dana watched from offstage as Emma eloquently stated her case against digitally distorted fashion photos.

———

Dana Edell was born in Hollywood, Florida, on November 28, 1975, a year and a half after her older sister, Erica. Her parents, Miriam and Steven, had met while working at a hospital in Philadelphia where her mother was a social worker and her father a radiologist. Dana's little sister was born not long after the family moved to Greenville, Delaware, a suburb of Philadelphia.

When Dana was four, both her older sister and her mother went to school. Miriam's pursuit of her dream to become a lawyer set an example for her daughters. At their synagogue and at home the girls were taught tolerance and the importance of supporting human rights. They played rough-and-tumble games with the boys next door, and they went camping and fishing with their dad. Dana didn't feel restricted being a girl until she reached high school when, as a teen girl, she was influenced by social stereotypes.

Throughout her youth Dana's parents had encouraged her love of the arts. When she was 12 they sent her to Interlochen Summer Arts Camp in northwest Michigan, hoping it would help her overcome her shyness. During her three summers there she found people like her among the fellow artists, musicians, and actors. During the last summer she attended the camp, she was part of a troupe that presented shows highlighting each performer's cultural background. By this time Dana had decided she would rather direct than act.

Dana loved Interlochen and wanted to attend the Interlochen Academy for the Arts, a boarding school for high school students. Uncertain of her parents' support for this wish, she submitted an application and was accepted without their knowledge. It wasn't until a bill arrived in the mail for the tuition that they knew anything about it. Used to their daughter's independence, they allowed her to attend. Dana's three years at Interlochen prepared her for Brown University in Providence, Rhode Island, and led to another experience that would set her on her life's path.

At Brown, Dana studied the classics and ancient Greeks, but it was her involvement with imprisoned women that changed her focus. Professor and playwright Paula Vogel ran a theater arts program for female inmates called SPACE (Space in Prison for Arts and Creative Expression). Dana joined other student volunteers in guiding women, ages 18 to 60, in self-expression through plays, poetry, and dance. Dana especially liked working with the younger inmates. During her senior year she and her friend Katie Eastburn launched a version of SPACE for girls. The juvenile hall in the nearby town of Cranston housed 300 inmates, of which only 25 were under 18. SPACE was the first recreational program offered to these girls, some of whom were incarcerated for prostitution and murder. Dance, drama, and poetry activities helped them express hopes, dreams, and fears. For girls who had suffered abuse and violence, the juvenile hall provided security, and SPACE helped them bond with each other and discover the power of collaboration to face negative experiences.

Healing emotional trauma through performing arts was powerful work for Dana. Neither she nor Katie felt ready to leave this work, but after graduating they were ready to go somewhere else and chose to move to San Francisco. There they started the Inside Out theater program with funds from a public service grant from Brown University. For the next two years they brought theater to girls at juvenile halls, homeless shelters, and group homes. Dana created an activity called the Slippery Jewel, about a jewel that bestowed good on anyone who held it. Survivors of incest and other sexual abuse would give this jewel to imagined abusers.

Katie left Inside Out to pursue her music career. With the grant funds depleted, Dana was struggling to keep the program operating alone. It seemed like the right time to go back to school to learn more directing skills. In 2000 Dana returned east to earn her MFA at Columbia University in New York. She loved living in the city and enjoyed her classes, but like many

New Yorkers her perspective shifted after the terrorist attack on September 11, 2001. Dana realized that she didn't want a career as a professional director. She missed working with girls. That autumn she directed a theater production about 9/11 with high school students in Harlem. By the following summer she and fellow student Chandra Thomas had created a summer theater project for Harlem teens and were able to use a theater and rehearsal stage at Columbia to put on a show performed by 18 neighborhood girls, titled *Say It How It Is*. At the girls' insistence they put on more productions. This was the beginning of the nonprofit organization viBe Theater.

During the following years Chandra and Dana facilitated more than 60 productions, with financial support from the city, corporations, and private foundations. In 2004 Katie rejoined Dana to supervise the music program and guided the girls in producing seven music CDs. Chandra, Katie, and Dana all believed in giving the girls the freedom and responsibility to make choices as a group in both choosing and implementing each project. One such group effort was the creation of a manual for young women covering sex, food, spirituality, and other topics. The guide included facts, resources, and activities for each subject.

Dana, Chandra, and Katie were more like shepherds than generals as they led their team of girls in discovering and developing their own voices. Meanwhile, after completing her master's in fine arts Dana entered New York University to earn a PhD in educational theater. Her work with viBe girls became the focus of her doctoral dissertation in which she documented how these urban girls both challenged and perpetuated their culture in their poetry and drama productions. Body image and sexuality were themes that appeared over and over. In 2007 when the American Psychological Association (APA) released a report on the sexualization of girls, Dana was excited by its content.

Using studies by noted social scientists and psychologists, the APA report documented how rampant sexualized images of girls and young women in advertising and the media damage the emotional and physical health of girls and can lead to depression, eating disorders, and low self-esteem. This was the first time a group of scholars had shown clear evidence of the danger of media portrayal of girls and young women as sex objects.

In October 2010 a coalition of organizations and researchers joined together at an event called the SPARK Summit to take action on the report's findings. Dana was there with them. One of the conference organizers, Hunter College professor Deborah Tolman, disputed media assertions that girls were not interested in sexualization and gender inequality, longtime issues for older feminists. She wrote, "We have news for those either glad or worried about this post-feminism nonsense: the Internet has become ground zero for feminist activism."

After the summit Tolman and Colby College professor and bestselling author Lyn Mikel Brown decided to use the energy generated at the summit to create a new organization called SPARK (Sexualization Protest: Action, Resistance, Knowledge) dedicated to empowering girls to push back against sexualization, gender bias, and objectification. With her vast experience working with girls, Dana was a natural choice for director of the program. Just like viBe Theater, SPARK would be a platform for girls to express their views and to demand and create change. With the help of a couple of staff members, Dana would coach a team of girl activists as they made choices about issues and actions to focus on. As director she would also be media spokesperson for SPARK.

Within a short time Dana was facilitating the work of 25 SPARK team activists living in different states and countries who stayed connected electronically through a private

Facebook group, conference calls, and a yearly retreat outside New York City. Her role as the adult was to mentor, provide editorial support for blogging, and develop a format for successful campaigns. Blog topics included fighting sexual harassment and assault on college campuses, the status of women in the media, intergenerational feminism, black women in TV and film, and dealing with rape culture. From 2011 to 2014 more than 300 pieces were posted on SPARK's blog site.

Some blog posts generated enough interest to become the focus of action, such as one against a Halloween costume called Anna Rexia. Dana helped put a petition online and later reported, "It was thrilling to witness how powerful we consumers actually are!" An online Halloween store "seemed to panic as soon as they noticed our petition accusing them of celebrating and sexualizing the leading cause of death for 15- to 24-year-old girls."

With help from the SPARK team, Dana, and other SPARK staffers, 13-year-old Julia Bluhm started a petition on Change.org asking *Seventeen* magazine to produce one photo spread a month without digital alteration of models. The 84,000 signatures caused the editor of *Seventeen* to take notice. In July 2012, Julia, then 14, wrote to her supporters, "*Seventeen* listened! They're saying they won't use Photoshop to digitally alter their models!" The media portrayed this victory as the act of a lone teen against a goliath company, but in reality Julia was the face of one protester backed by a team of girl activists and adult supporters.

Other prominent campaigns include one sparked by British team member Georgia Luckhurst's interview with Jennie Runk, a size 12 model featured in the H&M swimwear campaign. Jennie said, "When someone who is less than half your size calls herself fat, you end up questioning what you should be calling yourself. These kinds of conversations need to change." Georgia next joined team members Anya (in Michigan) and Montgomery (in New York City), in creating a campaign to get H&M to use plus-size mannequins in their stores by circulating a petition and asking activists to photograph girls posing as plus-size mannequins in H&M outlets.

Another SPARK campaign, this time for gender equality, began with the presentation of research and analysis of Google Doodles to Google executives. During the first three years that the site featured the doodles—illustrated images that decorate the search engine's main page—there was not one single doodle featuring a woman of color. And even though more than half the world's people are women, only 17 out of 100 doodles were of women.

SPARK wrote, "Google Doodles have become iconic and universal, and we believe that they should reflect the diversity of the world Google serves. As young women of color growing up in the United States, finding representations of ourselves in the media and elsewhere is tough. We want to hear the stories of people like us celebrated and told around the world."

Google responded to these issues by requesting that SPARK activists and Dana meet with their Doodle Us team. Presented with evidence of the imbalanced representation of women, a Doodle US team leader stated his intention to have men and women equally represented in future doodles. One Harvard clinical psychologist commented that SPARK activists were learning skills to "smart and outsmart really stupid stereotypes."

In a world where sexual images of young women inundate TV and print media, music videos, and film, the SPARK team and their coach Dana Edell have discovered ways to work together to grab media attention, mobilize opposition, and rally girls to join the fight against the sexualization of young women.

MALALA YOUSAFZAI

———◆———

Speaking Out for Girls' Education

"This is what my soul is telling me: be peaceful and love everyone." —Malala Yousafzai

---

In the midst of a battle between Afghan fighters and the British Army on May 27, 1880, the teenage daughter of a Pashtun shepherd became a great hero. While Malalai of Maiwand was tending the wounded at the edge of the battlefield, she noticed that the soldier bearing the Afghan flag had fallen. She raced onto the bloody field and raised the flag, rallying the Afghani warriors, among them her father and her betrothed. Before long, Malalai was also felled by a British bullet, and her brave death spurred the Afghanis on to victory. From that day Malalai of Maiwand has been celebrated as a Pashtun hero.

One hundred thirty-two years later, another Pashtun hero, Malala Yousafzai, stood before a special youth assembly of the United Nations on her 16th birthday, July 12, 2013. The UN had named it Malala Day in her honor; she declared that it was not just her day but one that belonged to every woman, boy, and girl who had spoken up for their rights.

"We realize the importance of our voice when we are silenced. In the same way, when we were in Swat, the north of Pakistan, we realized the importance of pens and books when we saw the guns. The wise saying, 'The pen is mightier than the sword.' It is true. The extremists are afraid of books and pens. The power of education frightens them. They are afraid of women. The power of the voice of women frightens them," Malala told the rapt audience. She ended the speech with a powerful call to action, "So let us wage a glorious struggle against illiteracy, poverty, and terrorism, let us pick up our books and our pens, they are the most powerful weapons." The audience of youth delegates and world leaders responded to her words with a thunderous standing ovation.

⸻

Among the Pashtun people of Afghanistan and Pakistan, the birth of a boy is celebrated with the firing of rifles and gifts from friends and family, while the birth of a girl is seldom rejoiced over. But Tor Pekai and Ziaudinn Yousafzai greeted the birth of their first child with joy. Ziaudinn, the new father, looked into his baby's eyes and sensed she would be someone special. And so she was named Malala in honor of Malalai of Maiwand.

Malala was born on July 12, 1997, in a two-room shack in Mingora, the main town in Swat Valley, Pakistan. Both her parents had grown up in tiny villages nestled in the mountain valley of Shangla. Ziaudinn was college educated and desperately wanted to establish his own school. Though Tor Pekai could neither read nor write, she admired his passion and steadfastly helped him to pursue this dream.

Ziaudinn was an eloquent, forceful speaker, but this skill had not come easily. As a boy he stuttered, and it seemed that becoming a well-known and respected orator like his father would be impossible. His mother had faith that Ziaudinn could overcome this barrier, and he did. Ziaudinn and Tor Pekai fell in love while Ziaudinn was studying at his uncle's house in the neighboring village. At first, Tor Pekai's father rejected the young man's offer of marriage, but months later he accepted when he knew Ziaudinn better.

As he tried to make his dream of starting a school a reality, Ziaudinn encountered many obstacles. He considered Malala to be his lucky charm because soon after her birth, his fortune changed. He became principal of Kushal School with 100 students, and the family moved from the shack into a roomy apartment on the school's second floor.

School was Malala's playground. The teachers were like aunts and uncles. Students were delighted when she toddled into the classroom. Malala was two years old when her brother was born. He was named Kushal, like the school, after a famous Pashtun warrior poet. Five years later their little brother, Atal, was born.

In 2001 the news of the terrorist attack on the World Trade Center in New York reached Swat Valley. Unknown to the people of Swat, this tragedy would turn their world upside down.

At the end of the Islamic month of Ramadan, during which Muslims go without eating each day from sunrise until sunset, comes a celebration to mark the end of fasting. Called Eid al-Fitr, this event marked the start of a school break. During this time, Malala's family traveled to visit family in the village of Shangla, boarding a bus called the Flying Coach for the bumpy four-hour journey on winding mountain roads.

WAR IN AFGHANISTAN

In 2001 NATO troops intervened in the conflict between the Afghan government and the Taliban, an extremist Islamic insurgent force. The goal of NATO was to capture Osama Bin Laden, the mastermind of the terrorist attack on September 11, 2001. The Taliban battled against the larger NATO forces using guerrilla raids, suicide bombings, and ambushes. The war spread to northwest Pakistan near Swat Valley in 2004. On May 2, 2011, US Navy SEALs assassinated Osama Bin Laden at his hideout in Pakistan. During this conflict tens of thousands of Afghani civilians died, as well as 10,000 Afghani soldiers and 4,000 foreign troops. As of March 2015 there were still 9,800 US troops in Afghanistan.

To Malala, Shangla seemed a forgotten place. Her cousins wore traditional handmade clothes, ran around barefoot, and had neither toys nor books. Every day they rose at dawn for the first of five daily prayers as the sun reflected off the high peak, Tor Ghar. Malala ran with her cousins through terraced fields and orchards past buffalo, butterflies, and bees. She feasted on walnuts and honey. Even though Mingora was tiny compared to real cities like Peshawar or Islamabad, her cousins thought of Malala as a city girl because she wore store-bought clothes and shoes.

On these visits Malala saw how women's lives were more restricted in Shangla than in Mingora. Here in the mountains women were confined to the part of the home known as purdah quarters. When going outside they had to cover their faces with a scarf. Speaking with any man who was not a close relative was forbidden, and flirting with a man was punishable by death. Women could even be used as payment to settle feuds between families.

When Malala expressed her dismay about these customs to her father he told her it was even worse in Afghanistan, where the Taliban burned girls' schools and forced women to wear a heavy head covering called a burqa. Furthermore they banned women from laughing in public and beat those that wore nail polish. Malala shivered in fear at the thought of living in such a place but took comfort in her father's words, "Malala is as free as a bird."

Malala was an excellent student, accustomed to being at the top of her class. She wept when a new girl in class earned higher grades. When she was seven years old Malala started stealing from a younger girl that she played with. After being caught with the loot, Malala first lied about her misdeed before admitting guilt. Seeing her in despair her father consoled her by quoting Mahatma Ghandi, "Freedom is not worth having if it does not include the freedom to make mistakes." Malala made a vow to never steal again. In the near future her family and community would see their freedoms taken away one by one, including the freedom to make mistakes.

The war in Afghanistan was now affecting Swat Valley. Thousands of young men had left the region to help the Taliban. Anti-American sentiments were growing and Islamic extremists became bolder. A self-appointed mufti, a religious scholar, living across the street started complaining to Ziaudinn about girls attending his school. Ziaudinn bravely defended the girls' right to an education.

On October 8, 2005, Malala was at school when a severe earthquake shook Pakistan. Kushal School survived, but students in other parts of the country were not so lucky. More than 18,000 died when their schools collapsed. In total almost 75,000 Pakistanis were killed. In remote Swat Valley most of the earthquake relief came from local groups, many affiliated with militant Islamic organizations. One such group was run by an extremist leader, Maulana Fazlullah, who claimed the earthquake was punishment for not following strict customs and Sharia law. The devastation of the earthquake created an opportunity for a takeover of the region by militant Muslims.

Malala was 10 years old when the Taliban, with their long straggly hair and beards and armed with knives and Kalashnikov rifles, came to Swat Valley. Fazlullah started a radio station to spread his teachings. At first he sounded reasonable,

SHARIA LAW

A group of Islamic laws based on the Koran, Sharia law includes discussions of duties, specific codes for behavior, and actions strictly forbidden in the Koran. Sharia law covers many aspects of life such as marriage, business, hygiene, sex, crime, and governance. Within the world's Islamic community there are many different interpretations of Sharia law and its current role in modern nations.

encouraging people to adopt better habits and abandon bad ones such as smoking and using drugs. Then he set down the law telling people not to listen to music, watch movies, or dance. In the streets Taliban soldiers torched piles of TVs, DVDs, and CDs. They broke into homes to confiscate any TVs they heard from the street. Malala and her brothers kept theirs hidden in a closet and only watched it with the volume set at low. Fazlullah banned women from appearing in public with their faces uncovered and from shopping in the bazaar. Anyone caught defying these decrees received a public whipping.

Next the killing started. The Taliban gunned down landowners, politicians, and policemen. One day a note was posted at the Kushal School gate threating punishment for Ziaudinn for running a Western-style school that educated girls. Ziaudinn fearlessly wrote a letter to the local newspaper, saying, "This is not the way to implement Islam. Please do not harm my children, because the God you believe in is the same God they pray to every day. You can take my life but please don't kill my schoolchildren." The Taliban started blowing up girls' schools nonetheless.

The sound of explosions was now common. One day while Malala was in her house there was a tremendous blast set off by a suicide bomber in the midst of a funeral for a popular local policeman. Several of her friends lost relatives in the explosion.

Ziaudinn continued to speak out against the Taliban. He and his friends traveled to Peshawar and Islamabad for interviews with foreign reporters. Malala also volunteered to be interviewed. Nervous at first, she became more confident the more she spoke with reporters.

Malala took on the name Gul Makai, meaning cornflower, in January 2009 when she started writing a diary published as a blog by the BBC (British Broadcasting Corporation). She wrote about her experience living in war-torn Swat Valley. Touched by her reports, newspapers around the world printed excerpts.

The Pakistan Army, which had been fighting the Taliban, was intensifying its attacks. Knowing there would soon be fighting in the streets of Mingora, townspeople started fleeing the city. Malala and her family joined the exodus. They returned to war-damaged Mingora after the army had declared Swat Valley safe. Within months the Taliban reappeared and resumed assassinations of their opponents.

In autumn 2011, Malala became even more visible when a *New York Times* reporter filmed a documentary about her. In December she received Pakistan's new National Peace Prize, called the Malala prize in her honor. Now she was in more danger than ever before. When the Taliban posted a death threat against Malala on the Internet, her parents wanted to send her away to boarding school in another part of the country. The police offered bodyguards. When Ziaudinn suggested the family cease their campaign, Malala responded, "You were the one who said if we believe in something greater than our lives, then our voices will only multiply if we are dead."

Each night Malala carefully bolted the main gate to her house. Spring and most of the summer passed without any incident. Then in August one of Ziaudinn's friends was wounded in an attack. Friends warned him that he might be next. On October 9, while Malala and other girls rode home on the school bus, two young men stepped out in the road forcing it to stop. They asked, "Who is Malala?" as they peered at the girls. Though all of them remained silent, one of the girls glanced at Malala. The last thing Malala remembered was the sound of gunshots. A bullet had passed through the left side of her face and entered her shoulder. Another girl had been struck in the left collarbone and palm, and a bullet grazed the right arm of a third girl. The shooters had quickly run away without being identified.

Malala's injury was the most serious. After being examined by doctors at the local hospital she was flown via helicopter to a hospital in Peshawar. Her brain was swelling. Surgeons removed a section of her skull and extracted the bullet from her shoulder. She was then raced off to Queen Elizabeth's Hospital in Birmingham, England, for operations to fix facial nerve damage and to protect her brain.

While she was in the hospital, thousands of gifts and cards arrived from people around the world, including Beyoncé and Angelina Jolie. Pakistan's president Zardari and former British prime minister Gordon Brown came to see her. Zardari said the government would pay her hospital bills. The president arranged for a place for her family to live in Birmingham, and

Malala Yousafzai meeting with President Obama, First Lady Michelle Obama, and daughter Malia Obama.
Official White House Photo / Pete Souza

he awarded Ziaudinn a job with the embassy. Malala missed her friends and home in Mingora, but she was thankful to attend school in Birmingham.

In March 2013 Malala was nominated for the Nobel Peace Prize, the youngest person ever to earn that honor. In July she spoke at the United Nations in New York and met with Queen Elizabeth at Buckingham Palace in London. In October she visited US president Barack Obama and boldly condemned the death of innocent Pakistanis from drone attacks. Her autobiography, *I Am Malala*, written with Christina Lamb, quickly became an international bestseller. As of 2014 it was still not for sale in Pakistan due to booksellers' fear of reprisals if they carried it in their stores.

Malala's campaign to protect the rights of girls to attend school in Swat had grown into a crusade to provide schooling for every child in the world. "One child, one teacher, one book and one pen," she says, "can change the world."

In October 2014 when the winners of that year's Nobel Peace Prize were announced, Malala was surprised to learn that she and Indian child rights activist Kailash Satyarthi would share the prize. Malala said she was encouraged by the award and the support of so many people to carry on her work. She said the award was not only for her but all the children who are voiceless, and she encouraged her fellow youth to stand up for their rights.

PART II

RISING UP AGAINST GREED

MARY HARRIS
"MOTHER" JONES

—◆—

The Queen of Agitators

"My address is like my shoes: it travels with me. I abide where there is a fight against wrong." —Mother Jones

---

I n August 1899 when striking coal miners in Arnot, Pennsylvania, were ready to call it quits, a white-haired woman known as Mother Jones came to the rescue. Though she looked like a frail old grandmother, she made mine bosses tremble. Her words energized demoralized workers. The company bosses did not want her in Arnot. On their orders the innkeeper refused her lodging. After a miner and his family hosted her in their cabin for the night, the mine bosses evicted them from the company-owned housing. Undaunted, Mother Jones arrived with the family at a miners rally. Her tale of their heartless eviction enraged the miners and reignited their fighting spirit.

The mine bosses brought in nonunion workers, known as scabs, to keep the mines in operation. Mother Jones ordered the men to stay home to care for the children and organized the women for the battle. She chose a fiery red-haired Irishwoman as their commander, and she sent the women off to the mine equipped with dishpans and spoons. When the redhead saw the sheriff leading a crew of scabs and a string of mules, she whacked him over the head with her dishpan. Then the ruckus began. The clanging of dishpans and howls of wild women spooked the mules, sending them bucking back to the barn. The scabs scurried away, pursued by women as furious as a swarm of hornets. They dared not return to the mine as long as the women were on guard. With the mines out of operation, the company finally conceded to the union's demands.

Ellen and Richard Harris's second child, Mary, was born in late July 1837 at their home in Cork, Ireland. Following Mary came two more daughters. By 1846, when Mary's little brother was born, the Irish were suffering from a great famine that would claim one million lives. Thousands of evicted farmers arrived in port cities, like Cork, to board ships to other countries. The next year, Richard and Richard Junior joined the exodus to North America in search of work. During the years they waited for Richard to send for them, Mary and her family witnessed mass starvation and death.

Mary's father and brother found jobs laying railroad track. Within five years they saved enough money to bring the rest of the family to Canada, where they settled in Toronto. Their small house sat on a lot big enough to stable five cows and grow a large garden. Here, teenage Mary learned the craft of dressmaking.

At the age of 20 she entered a teacher-training course at Toronto Normal School and soon was qualified to teach.

Mary was anxious to set off on her own. In 1859 she moved to Michigan to teach at a convent school, but she only stayed for half a year before heading off to Chicago to work briefly as a dressmaker. She moved on to Memphis, Tennessee, by 1860 where she set up a shop.

In Memphis she met and married an iron molder named George Jones. He earned a good enough living making casts for iron products that Mary could quit working. By June 1861, the Civil War had begun, and Tennessee had seceded from the Union. The next year Union forces captured Memphis. During the occupation Mary and George's first child, Catherine, was born. While battles raged elsewhere in Tennessee, life in Memphis remained relatively safe and prosperous. Before the war's end, Mary gave birth to two more children. Their fourth child arrived just before her life crumbled.

"In 1867, a fever epidemic swept Memphis. . . . Across the street from me, ten persons lay dead from the plague. The dead surrounded us. They were buried at night quickly and without ceremony. . . . One by one, my four little children sickened and died. I washed their little bodies and got them ready for burial. My husband caught the fever and died. I sat alone through nights of grief. No one came to me. No one could. Other homes were as stricken as was mine. All day long, all night long, I heard the grating of the wheels of the death cart," wrote Mary Harris Jones.

It would have been natural for Mary to be paralyzed with grief, but it was the needs of others that kept her going. She remained in Memphis nursing the sick until the plague was over.

Mary returned to the life of a dressmaker in Chicago. Working with a partner, she served Chicago's wealthy class. "Often while sewing for the lords and barons who lived in magnificent houses on the Lake Shore Drive, I would look out of the plate glass windows and see the poor, shivering wretches, jobless and hungry, walking along the frozen lake front. The contrast of their condition with that of the tropical comfort of the people for whom I sewed was painful to me. My employers seemed neither to notice nor to care," she recounted.

Over the next four years Mary's business prospered, and then tragedy struck again. In October 1871 her dress shop and home, along with all her worldly possessions, burned in the Great Chicago Fire. As she did before, Mary chose not to dwell on her loss but instead focused on those less fortunate. Over the next two decades as Mary rebuilt her business she learned about the miserable conditions of workers and the greed of industrial barons. These were times of wide swings between prosperity and depression during which the poor suffered the most. The financial panic of 1874 left one million workers without jobs.

Worker protests and rallies were violently repressed in cities like Chicago, which in turn planted seeds for militancy among union members and political radicals. In 1883 there were more mass protests, followed by another economic depression that lasted for years. By 1886 labor unions were demanding an eight-hour workday—in that era, many workdays lasted more than 15 hours. On May 1 of that year 300,000 workers walked off their jobs. Police, militias, and hired thugs savagely attacked worker rallies and marches. In 1893 a third financial collapse left tens of thousands unemployed. While workers were continually losing their jobs and having wages cut, the rich got richer. Mary had been married to a union man, and she wanted to join the cause. Her chance soon arrived.

In 1894 Jacob Coxey, who owned a small business in Ohio, led a march of jobless workers to Washington, DC, to demand

UNIONS

During the industrial revolution, craft guilds (associations of skilled craftspeople and artisans) declined in number, and factory, mill, and mine workers were forced to accept low wages, long work shifts, unsafe conditions, and abuse from bosses. A single worker had no power, but in trade unions, workers could band together to make demands. When bosses refused to negotiate, workers could walk off the job en masse and shut down production. This tactic is called a strike. Often bosses would employ nonunion workers, called scabs, to keep production going.

jobs fixing roads, bridges, and other public works. In Mary's first labor action, she volunteered to collect money and food for his followers, dubbed Coxey's Army by the press. Her rousing speeches buoyed morale. Once the marchers reached Washington, the police disbanded the group. The government ignored their demands, but Coxey's Army had captured the public's interest and set forth an idea that became reality during the Great Depression with the creation of public works jobs for the unemployed. At age 57, Mary Jones took on the name Mother Jones. In this persona she spoke with workers as one of them, in their own jargon. The combination of her motherly appearance, dressed in old-fashioned black clothes, and her fearless verbal attacks on the rich, soon earned her notoriety as a labor leader. As a mother who had lost her own children she became a mother to many.

Now Mary, as Mother Jones, lived wherever her shoes took her. Wandering from mill to mine she rallied workers to claim their power. Her successful support of miners in Arnot, Pennsylvania, was followed by her arrest in West Virginia for organizing striking miners. At her trial, a US district attorney called her "the most dangerous woman in America" because of her skill at inciting workers to strike. Worried about making her a martyr and multiplying her power, the judge suspended her sentence of two months in jail.

In 1901 Mother Jones worked in the textile mills in the South, where barefoot boys and girls walked up and down aisles for hours reaching into machinery to repair broken threads. Day and night they replaced spindles and squirmed underneath the machines to squirt oil. Some even operated machinery specially built for the size of a child. Six-year-olds worked eight hours for 10 cents, while younger siblings helping them were paid nothing. Injuries were common. Mother Jones met one girl

WORKING CONDITIONS IN COAL MINES

Working in coal mines was a dangerous job. In the late 19th century thousands of miners perished in tunnel collapses, explosions, and other accidents. Others died from black lung disease. Miners suffered from long shifts and low pay. Living in towns where most stores and housing were owned by coal companies, workers were forced to pay high rents and prices for food.

in Tuscaloosa who later died when her hair was caught in the whirring machinery. Many children perished from pneumonia.

"At five-thirty in the morning long lines of little grey children came out of the early dawn into the factory, into the maddening noise and lint filled rooms. Outside the birds sang and the blue sky shone," wrote Mother.

Factories ignored laws banning child labor. The more Mother Jones saw, the more outraged she became. Her anger turned to action while she was in Pennsylvania assisting the 75,000 mill workers striking for higher wages and shorter hours. Of them at least 10,000 were children.

"Every day little children came into Union Headquarters, some with their hands off, some with the thumb missing, some with their fingers off at the knuckle. They were stooped little things, round shouldered and skinny," she remembered.

When Mother Jones questioned newspaper reporters about the absence of stories about these child laborers, they said they could not write anything because the mills owned stock in the papers. "Well I've got stock in these little children," she responded, "And I'll arrange a little publicity."

It was time to bring the issue to the president. With the help of parents and volunteers Mother Jones organized the March of the Mill Children. With each child wearing a knapsack containing a knife, fork, tin cup, and plate, they set off from Philadelphia for Theodore Roosevelt's home in Oyster Bay, New York. To the sound of two small children playing a drum and fife, children strode along bearing banners stating, "We want time to play" and "Prosperity is here. Where is ours?" For the first time in their lives these children were outside of the gloomy mills, trekking under the open skies, bathing in brooks, and feasting on food donated by farmers. Except for the many miles they had to walk, it was almost like a vacation.

CHILD LABOR TODAY

It wasn't until 1938 that federal laws prohibited children under the age of 16 from working in factories, mills, and mines, though farm labor was excluded. Today, as many as 500,000 children work on American farms. Long shifts of 10 hours or more, the use of sharp tools, and exposure to extreme heat and harmful pesticides are responsible for high rates of injuries and deaths for these children. Worldwide 168 million children toil in factories, fields, and mines contributing to the manufacture of low-cost products available for sale.

In New York City Mother Jones spoke to a large crowd about the horrors of child labor and introduced injured and prematurely aged child workers. At Coney Island the children were treated to a wild animal show. When they reached the gates of President Roosevelt's mansion, he refused to meet with them, but the Crusade of the Mill Children had brought attention to their plight.

Over the next decade Mother Jones traveled from Colorado to West Virginia, Michigan, and New York aiding striking mine, mill, and garment factory workers. Year by year her legend grew, and people sung her praises. One woman union organizer wrote that Mother Jones had a "voice whose call I could follow to the end of the road." Another wrote, "She is indeed their mother in word and deed. She has earned the sweetest of all names honestly."

In September 1913 Mother Jones, now 76 years old, arrived in Trinidad, Colorado, to organize miners for a strike after the coal companies rejected their demands for shorter shifts, higher pay, safer conditions, the elimination of mine guards, and the right to unionize. When workers walked off their jobs, company guards forced them out of their homes. They settled into temporary colonies of tents supplied by the union. Mother Jones rallied the strikers to demonstrate and persevere in the face of harsh conditions and intimidation.

General Chase of the Colorado National Guard illegally banned Mother Jones from Trinidad. When she defied his order she was deported to Denver. She was deported again when she returned. After returning to Trinidad for the third time she was held prisoner at a convent hospital for nine weeks until she was released under pressure from union lawyers. During her next attempt to visit the striking miners, soldiers boarded the train before it reached Trinidad. She was confined in a cell in the basement of a courthouse that had previously been ruled unfit for habitation by prisoners.

"It was a cold, terrible place, without heat, damp and dark. I slept in my clothes by day and at night and fought sewer rats with a beer bottle. 'If I were out of this dungeon,' thought I, 'I would be fighting the human sewer rats anyway!'"

She was released but never allowed to return to Trinidad. On April 20, 1914, while she was gone from the region, troops and mine guards massacred 19 people at Ludlow Colony. More than half of the dead were women and children. Though the event caught the public's attention, the killers were never arrested.

Mother Jones continued to fight for workers' rights for 10 more years. Workers called her the Miner's Angel. In the US

Mother Jones with President Calvin Coolidge, First Lady Grace Anna
Coolidge, and Theodore Roosevelt Jr., in 1924.
Courtesy of Library of Congress LC-USZ62-73975

Senate, she had been called the "grandmother of all agitators."
To this epithet she replied that her wish was to one day be the
"great-grandmother of all agitators."

Some people lie about their age to appear younger. Mary
Harris "Mother" Jones did the opposite. At some point in her
life she changed her birth date to 1830, adding seven years to
her age. As Mother Jones she celebrated her "100th birthday"
(actually just shy of her 93rd) on May 1, 1930, at a party that
featured music by a band composed of elderly former soldiers,

a delegation of hobos, a cake made by union bakers, and union leaders, politicians, and friends. She made her first recording on a phonograph record saying, "And I long to see the day when Labor will have the destiny of the nation in her own hands."

Six months later Mother Jones passed away. As she wished, she was buried in the Union Miners Cemetery. On the 22-foot-tall memorial at her gravesite, graced with her image, are the words "Pray for the Dead and Fight Like Hell for the Living."

VANDANA SHIVA

———◆———

Food and Forests for the People

"You do not measure the fruit of your actions. You have to measure the obligation of your actions. You have to find out what's the right thing to do. That is your duty. Whether you win or lose is not the issue." —Vandana Shiva

---

Vandana Shiva and a group of peasant women each embraced a tree trunk in an effort to prevent loggers from chopping them down.

This tactic had first been used in the mountains of Uttarakhand, India, on March 26, 1974, to save another forest from destruction. Led by a woman in her fifties named Gaura Devi, a group of 27 women and girls from the village of Reni had stopped the destruction of their forest. "Brothers! This forest is the source of our livelihood. If you destroy it, the mountain will come tumbling down onto our village," Gaura proclaimed. She stood in front of the gun held by one of the loggers and she stated, "This forest nurtures us like a mother; you will only be able to

Vandana Shiva.
Courtesy of Kartikey Shiva

use your axes on it if you shoot me first." Despite threats and abuse from the loggers, the women held their ground; their whole existence as a people was connected to the forest. The loggers, who were also mountain people, listened and eventually backed off.

This action was pivotal to the peasant movement called Chipko (the Hindi word meaning "to stick to") in achieving government protection of forests in the Himalayas. Vandana grew up exploring these forests with her father. Her favorite spot was a cascading stream where her family enjoyed swimming. She believed that the streams and forests near her home in the Doon Valley would exist forever.

Years later, after returning home on a vacation from university studies in Canada, Vandana discovered that not only was her favorite spot gone, but the whole forest had vanished as well. In its place was a massive orchard funded by the World Bank. On future school breaks, Vandana stood in solidarity with the peasant women to halt the deforestation. Being in the forest, being in the company of wise mountain women, transformed Vandana and shifted her life's journey.

═══════

Vandana Shiva was born on November 5, 1952, in Dehradun, the capital of the north Indian state of Uttarakhand. Living at the lower end of the long, broad Doon Valley, Vandana grew up surrounded by dramatic vistas of the Himalaya Mountains. Her mother had graduated from school in Lahore, a rarity in her generation that gave her the privilege of serving as an inspector of schools. In 1947, after the partition of India, Lahore was in the new country of Pakistan. Vandana's mother chose to abandon her career to become a farmer in India. For many years she involved herself politically supporting the new India, the largest democracy in the world. In actions and words, she nurtured Vandana's power and wisdom.

"She has always been a major influence for me in never feeling second rate because you're born a woman, never feeling afraid of any circumstance in life. I never saw her afraid, and yet, with all that, she was so deeply compassionate. She taught that if anyone needs you, you should be available to them," said Vandana about her mother.

Both of Vandana's parents possessed a passion for nature. Her mother wrote about the spiritual aspect of nature. Her father worked as a forest conservationist. Vandana spent endless hours outdoors with him while he passed on his love and knowledge of forests. She also shared with her parents an admiration for Mahatma Gandhi, the great nonviolent activist who helped end British colonial rule.

At the age of nine, Vandana admired the famous physicist Albert Einstein. By the time she was a teenager she had decided to become a physicist like him. To be admitted to a university physics program she would need to take high school physics and high-level math courses. Since her high school didn't offer these classes, Vandana studied these subjects on her own, scored well on college admission tests, and was accepted to the University of Guelph in Ontario, Canada.

Vandana thrived at university. She earned a bachelor's degree in science and then went on to receive a master's degree. At the University of Western Ontario, halfway between Toronto and Detroit, Vandana pursued her PhD. Her studies caused her to question the structure of the world. Vandana now viewed the physical world as one, where everything is connected. She had not foreseen when she had decided to study physics that it would bring her full circle to her youthful passion for the natural world. She realized that most people studied science by viewing everything in the universe in isolation. Her passion now centered on what she calls "real science," the science of interconnection. She realized that small farmers in India use their knowledge of interrelationships between soil, water, pollinators, herbivores, and plants to successfully grow crops.

Back in India, Vandana returned to her work with Chipko activists, with whom she had initially connected through her parents. Her father was one of the few forestry officials who supported their efforts to protect the forest. Vandana observed that streams and springs were drying up as a result of logging and clearing forests for massive agricultural projects. She knew that people living in the mountains had to walk farther and farther for fresh water. She learned that the removal of trees, which hold the soils together, caused increased flooding and landslides. One flood in 1978 eroded an entire mountain. The debris dammed a section of the Ganges River, forming a lake. When the dam burst, there was a massive flood that inundated whole neighborhoods in Calcutta hundreds of miles away.

Officials in the Indian government now saw the truth in what the Chipko activists had been saying. As Vandana's relationships with village women grew closer, she too realized that they had a deeper knowledge of the forest than her scientifically trained father. Now a student at a different kind of school, she observed and listened, absorbing their wisdom.

As a university graduate Vandana saw she had a special role to play. Government officials viewed Chipko activists as illiterate villagers. She could use her education to assist the villagers in writing reports that officials would pay attention to. Vandana started an organization, the Research Foundation for Science, Technology, and Ecology. With her office in her mother's cowshed and start-up funds from her parents, Vandana set to work supporting the activists. On each issue, she provided them with the scientific facts and figures necessary to counter the arguments of their opponents.

Vandana was learning about the kind of power manifested by women standing up fearlessly to block destructive forces. Day by day she saw how the knowledge of illiterate peasant women was so often dismissed because of their lack of scientific education, when in reality the women's traditional knowledge enabled them see the big picture. In the 1980s massive limestone quarrying was occurring in the Doon Valley. When asked what the biggest issue was, the women villagers simply replied, "water." They knew that cavities in the limestone were the source of the valley's abundant water. They knew something none of the scientists had mentioned. Vandana reported their knowledge in terms that science-literate officials could understand.

Vandana became concerned about the survival of centuries-old traditional farming techniques and crops. In 1991 she established Navdanya, an organization dedicated to assisting farmers in rescuing and conserving crops and plants on the verge of extinction. Its mission also included preserving and reviving indigenous knowledge and culture, defending crops that had been developed by farmers over millennia from biopiracy, and educating the people about the hazards of genetically modified crops. To rescue the rich diversity of India's crops, the organization began a program of seed saving. Within 25 years Navdanya had conserved more than 5,000 varieties of crops, including 3,000 of rice and 150 varieties of wheat.

In March 1995 an American medical center was granted a patent by the US Patent Office for "inventing" medicinal uses of turmeric. This plant has been used for thousands of years for healing wounds and rashes. The patent would prevent anyone except the medical center from selling turmeric for this medical use. One by one, plants that were part of India's cultural and economic heritage were patented, including the neem tree, known as "nature's drugstore." Growing throughout South Asia, the tree provides pesticide, food, and medicines for a wide variety

BIOPIRACY

Throughout time, across the world, people have used medicines, pesticides, and other products derived from local plants and other organisms. By the 1990s an increasing number of businesses or institutions were claiming the ownership, through the legal process of patenting, of a medical or other use of naturally occurring plants or other organisms. These patents disregarded the traditional uses of these plants by cultures throughout the world. This theft of folk uses of organisms is known as biopiracy.

of ailments. In 1997 the patent for turmeric was revoked, but as of 2014 patents for more than a dozen other plants used in India were still intact. Vandana and other activists hoped to revoke these patents by changing patent laws.

"The statement that this kind of piracy is an 'invention' is a bit like the statement that Columbus was the first to 'discover' this country [the United States]. In fact, this country was 'discovered' over millennia by the Native Americans," argued Vandana.

Vandana wrote about biopiracy and the patenting of genetically engineered seeds in her book *Stolen Harvest*, published in 2000. In it she issued a warning about the hijacking of the world's food supply by a few large corporations. The biggest villain in her sights was Monsanto, which had been aggressively taking control of the seed industry until it became the largest seed company in the world. Eventually it controlled more than 90 percent of the cotton and soy production in India using GMO (genetically modified organism) seeds.

Until the mid-1990s there had been no corporate involvement in India's food system. India's laws protected small farmers, land rights, and market prices so that small farmers could make a living. Then globalization laws and treaties granted more power to corporations. These new rules were devised by the businesses that would profit most and that had enough political power to have them approved by governments.

Shortly after the turn of the century genetically modified cotton was planted in India. It was advertised as a miracle plant that would not require pesticides or herbicides because it contained, through the insertion of bacteria, genes that were harmful to some insect pests. Most of the small farmers who bought Monsanto genetically modified seeds had not realized that plants from these new seeds would require irrigation, the use

GENETICALLY MODIFIED ORGANISMS

When the genetic blueprint of an organism is changed by inserting DNA, cloning, or synthesizing DNA, the organism is known to be genetically modified. Numerous organisms, from bacteria and yeasts to higher life forms such as insects, fish, mammals, and plants, have been altered through this process. If a genetically modified organism is considered commercially valuable, the inventor can apply for patents. Concerns about genetic engineering include creation of new food allergens, genetic contamination of other food crops, and the death of animals such as Monarch butterflies from genes from insect diseases inserted into genetically modified crops. By 2013 more than 60 countries around the world, including Australia, Japan, and all of the countries in the European Union, had significant restrictions or bans on the production and sale of GMOs.

of more pesticides, and chemical fertilizers. By 2009 research showed that Monsanto's GMO cottonseeds were no longer effective against the pests that the company had guaranteed protection from. Production levels fell. Farmers saddled with debts incurred from the increased costs of irrigation, pesticides, and herbicides saw their incomes plummet. By 2011 more than a quarter million farmers had committed suicide.

Vandana let the world know about this tragedy.

"The farmer suicides started in 1997. That's when the corporate seed control started," Vandana Shiva told CNN's Christiane Amanpour. "And it's directly related to indebtedness, and indebtedness created by two factors linked to globalization." Those two factors were the control of India's seed supply by the corporate chemical industry, which led to higher production costs for financially vulnerable, struggling farmers, coupled with falling prices in a global agricultural economy.

"The poorest families, the poorest children, are subsidizing the growth of the largest agribusinesses in the world," said Vandana. She then added that Monsanto "is making money by coercing and literally forcing people to pay for what was free."

Vandana warns the people of the world of a future where access to the basic necessities of life, water, and food will be controlled by a small number of massive multinational corporations. Also in their control would be national governments meant to serve their citizens but instead hijacked by corporate money. Vandana says the way to escape such a future is to practice "Earth democracy."

"All members of the earth community, including all humans, have the right to sustenance—to food and water, to a safe and clean habitat, to security of ecological space. Resources vital to sustenance must stay in the commons. The right to sustenance is a natural right because it is the right to life. States or corporations do not give these rights, nor can they be extinguished by state or corporate action. No state or corporation has the right to erode or undermine these natural rights or enclose the commons that sustain life," writes Vandana in her book *Earth Democracy*.

When once asked if she had fun traveling the world to crusade against injustice, Vandana replied, "I do have fun. Even when I'm fighting I'm enjoying it, for two reasons: I think there's nothing as exhilarating as protecting that which you find precious. To me, fighting for people's rights, protecting nature, protecting diversity, is a constant reminder of that which is so valuable in life."

RIGOBERTA MENCHÚ TUM

———◆———

Touched by the Hand of Destiny

"What I treasure most in life is being able to dream. During my most difficult moments and complex situations I have been able to dream of a more beautiful future."
—*Rigoberta Menchú Tum*

Rigoberta Menchú Tum knew sadness at a young age. When she was nine years old, her two-year-old brother Nicolas died from malnutrition. And before she was born her oldest brother Felipe had died after being sprayed with pesticide as he picked cotton. Both these tragedies occurred while her family was working on plantations in the lowlands of Guatemala harvesting crops. After Nicolas died, her mother took the day off to bury him and was fired from her job. The boss ordered her to leave the finca (plantation) and refused to pay her for the two weeks that she had worked that month. Rigoberta later said of this event, "I remember it with enormous hatred." But after working hard as an activist her attitude changed. She

Mural of Rigoberta Menchú at the Batahola Cultural Center in Managua, Nicaragua.
Mural © Gerardo Hernández, photo courtesy of Andrea Kraybill

began to feel that "hatred is a disease of the spirit, and I don't want to be sick."

Rigoberta Menchú Tum was born on January 9, 1959, in the hamlet of Chimel in the highlands of Guatemala, to Vicente Menchú and Juana Tum. She was their sixth child. Poor peasants of Mayan heritage, Rigoberta's parents and the family were the first to settle in what would become Chimel. Despite being materially impoverished, Vicente and Juana felt wealthy farming on their community's land in the mountains. Unfortunately the poor soil and cool climate made it difficult to grow enough crops to supply them with adequate food and income. Over the years they knew the soil would slowly improve, but until then they had to migrate to the lowlands for part of the year to earn money working on fincas.

The cloud-shrouded mountains were beautiful and home to a wide variety of plants useful for food, medicines, and building materials. In remote Chimel the people were free to practice sacred customs. Each family taught their children to respect family, community, and Mother Earth. Each child learned about their *nahual*, a protective spirit that would accompany them through their life.

From a young age Rigoberta was a good helper. She assisted her mother in mixing *nixtamal*, the dough used to make tamales and tortillas from the maize (corn), and looked after her younger siblings. Tending to the crops on their own land in the highlands was hard but sometimes joyous work. By the age of nine Rigoberta was wielding an axe and machete to chop firewood. She hauled water from more than a mile away with other girls. She joined the same girls on treks up the mountainsides to gather leaves used for tamales. Even though they were working, they had fun laughing and singing together.

She felt sadness each year when her family left their little house in the mountains to work on a finca, where they slept in a large unwalled structure among 300 or more other people. Most of the other farm workers were Mayan, but they were from different parts of Guatemala and conversed in different dialects than K'iché (kee-chay), which people in the Chimel region spoke.

On the fincas the bosses who supervised the workers were often abusive. They cheated workers out of pay and skimped on money for making the meals. Not only were the cooks forced to serve meager portions, meals were often made out of spoiled ingredients. If workers complained about any of these injustices they would be fired and the pay owed them would be pocketed by the boss. In the fincas Rigoberta witnessed her people being treated without respect, a complete contrast to how the people in Chimel behaved with each other.

On the fincas, Rigoberta's mother, Juana, worked hard preparing meals for fellow farm workers. The first meal was at three o'clock in the morning before they went to work, the next at midday, and the last at seven in the evening. When she wasn't cooking, she harvested coffee. Rigoberta and the other children helped Juana pick the coffee berries, but Rigoberta didn't receive pay for this work until she was eight years old, when she set herself the task of picking 35 pounds of coffee a day to earn 20 centavos (less than a nickel in US currency).

When Rigoberta turned 10 years old, she had her coming-of-age ceremony in Chimel. Her mother and father explained the responsibilities of adulthood. At age 12 her father gave her a small pig, two chickens, and a lamb to care for on her own. Rigoberta especially loved the lamb. Though these animals were not pets, when the time came to kill them for food the slaughter would be preceded by prayers of thanks. In addition to practicing Mayan ceremonies most families in Chimel also practiced Catholicism. Rigoberta and other youngsters learned Catholic doctrine from visiting priests, who also taught her Spanish.

By the mid-1970s the farms in Chimel were beginning to produce bountiful crops. In Guatemala the rich were not only used to controlling the government but also felt they had the right to take whatever they wanted from the impoverished Mayan people. When a group of wealthy landowners living near Chimel

MAYAN PEOPLE

With roots in the Mayan civilization that dominated Central America for centuries before the arrival of the Spanish, contemporary Mayan people occupying the area share similar customs and diverse dialects of the Mayan language group. Guatemala has the largest Mayan population of Central America.

became aware of the increased fertility of Chimel's farms, they falsely claimed that they owned the land, convinced that they could steal it from the families, including Rigoberta's family.

What these landowners hadn't counted on was resistance. The community chose Rigoberta's father, Vicente, to lead the defense of the people's land. Vicente traveled to the nation's capital, Guatemala City, to take their case to the government. Like most people in Chimel, he was unable to read or write, and he was an easy target for corrupt officials. The officials drew up a document that, instead of confirming the community's land right as they told Vicente, actually promised to give it away after two years to the people trying to steal it.

In response to the community's refusal to abandon their land, the wealthy landowners hired thugs who violently evicted the people from their homes and drove them out of the village. In the process they also stole valuables, broke kitchenware, scattered stores of corn, and slaughtered both livestock and dogs. With nowhere else to live, the villagers camped out together for 40 days before they decided to risk returning to their homes to gather cooking utensils and corn. Supplied with pots and other needed items from people in a nearby village, they settled back into their houses.

The wealthy landowners told them they could stay in their homes but they would have to abandon ownership of their land, which would become part of a big finca on which the villagers could work as laborers. Vicente refused this offer, choosing to fight the theft of his community's land. After the village was raided once again, they camped out in the forest before returning to their homes once more.

Just before Rigoberta turned 13 she accepted a job as a maid for a wealthy family in Guatemala City, where she was treated with less respect than the family dog and cheated out of her pay. Around her 14th birthday one of her brothers arrived in the city to tell her that their father was in prison. She abandoned her job without any hesitation and returned home to help her mother free Vicente.

It took 14 months, but they got Vicente released from prison. The landlords were so furious that he was free that they hired ruffians to abduct him. They beat him severely and left him to die. During the months-long recovery, Vicente received word that he would be abducted again. With the help of local priests and nuns he was moved to a safe location where he could recover.

Though he had difficulty walking, Vicente continued traveling. Someone always accompanied him, usually Rigoberta. From village to village they went, meeting with peasants suffering similar repression. During this time he was arrested again and released. From that time on he traveled and organized secretly, and he helped form the Committee of Unified Campesinas (CUC), an organization dedicated to the resistance of peasants to land theft and repression.

In Chimel, Rigoberta joined her community in devising plans for defense against future raids. These included pit traps, taking turns as sentries, and designating escape routes. Soon she was visiting other communities on behalf of the CUC, assisting the people in setting up self-defense measures.

In May 1978 the Guatemalan army massacred 106 people in the town of Panzós, where oil had been discovered, after the people defied the army's order to abandon their land. The CUC condemned the murders, but the situation only became worse when a new president, Luis Garcia, came into power. There were more massacres. In September 1979 Rigoberta's younger brother, Petrocinio, was one of 21 men abducted and then brutally tortured and killed. These horrific deeds only cemented the villagers' resolve to resist.

At the end of January peasants and students marched in the capital to publicize the army's kidnapping and murder of villagers in Uspantán. Vicente Menchú was in a group that entered the embassy of Spain, a country sympathetic to their plight, to hold a press conference. In the ensuing attack by police, a fire broke out that killed 36 people, among them Spanish diplomats and Guatemalan activists, including Vicente Menchú.

Less than three months later, the army kidnapped Rigoberta's mother, tortured her, and left her to die. It was a terrible end for someone like Juana Tum, who had lived a pure life full of kindness for others. Rigoberta and her siblings knew if they went to recover her body and bury it they too would be tortured and murdered.

Rigoberta decided not to join the guerrilla army as her sisters did. Knowing that the army was hunting for her, she stayed in hiding until fleeing to Mexico in 1981. That year about 35,000 peasants were slaughtered and another several hundred thousand were driven from their homes in the Guatemalan

GUATEMALAN CIVIL WAR

In 1954, Colonel Carlos Castillo Armas overthrew the democratically elected president of Guatemala, Jacobo Arbenz, in a coup supported by the US Central Intelligence Agency. In the rabid anticommunist 1950s, Arbenz was demonized by the United States for legalizing the Communist Party and proposing to take over plantations of the United Fruit Company, a business that virtually ruled Central America. Armas immediately reversed land reforms and voting rights for impoverished Mayan peasants, returning them to near-slave status. By 1960 left-wing insurgents had begun resisting the army, beginning a 36-year war between the common people and the wealthy elite and army.

highlands. During the years of conflict, 200,000 villagers perished, 400 Indian villages were destroyed, and more than 38,000 people disappeared.

As a political refugee Rigoberta soon became known through her speeches and interviews. In 1982 she narrated her life story to Venezuelan anthropologist and author Elizabeth Burgos. The book *I, Rigoberta Menchú* was soon translated into five other languages. It not only alerted the world to the plight of her people, it also made her a symbol of brave resistance.

Despite the threat of death, Rigoberta returned to Guatemala to work with different organizations, such as the CUC and the Vicente Menchú Revolutionary Christians, a group named in honor of her father. She narrated the film *When the Mountains Tremble*, which was made by a US production company. The film won awards at film festivals and further focused the spotlight on Rigoberta and her people's plight.

Rigoberta now traveled throughout Europe telling her people's story. In 1992 she had to decide which of 260 international invitations to accept, including one from the prime minister of Austria and another from the queen of England. In December 1992 she became the youngest and the first indigenous woman to win the Nobel Peace Prize.

"We have broken the silence around Guatemala," Rigoberta Menchú remarked after receiving the prize. "Now I would like to see Guatemala at peace, with indigenous and nonindigenous people living side-by-side. . . . We indigenous people, not just the Guatemalan people, deserve this prize. It is a gift of life, a gift for history, and a gift of our time."

In response to her petition to the United Nations to give organizations representing dispossessed people a forum to speak at the UN, they declared 1993 the International Year of Indigenous Populations. With her more than one million dollars of peace prize money, Rigoberta helped establish the Rigoberta Menchú Tum Foundation to help Guatemalan exiles return home, as well as to monitor the government's treatment of indigenous communities.

In 1994 Rigoberta married Angel Canil, whose family she had become very close to. They had two children; the second died shortly after birth. Feeling shielded from death squads by her Nobel Peace Prize she returned to her homeland, but she moved to Mexico City after she received more threats on her life.

Finally on December 29, 1996, a peace accord negotiated by the UN was signed, ending 36 years of terror. In a strange twist of fate, Guatemala's new president, Oscar Berger, invited Rigoberta to return home to serve as goodwill ambassador to the

Rigoberta Menchú in a march commemorating the anniversary of the signing of a treaty on Identity and Rights of Indigenous Peoples.
Wikimedia Commons

peace accords. Here a man from a family of wealthy landowners was looking for help from a peasant who could have once toiled on one of his plantations.

Rigoberta was ready to help, but she was also intent on bringing to justice those people who were responsible for the deaths of not just her mother, father, and brother but also of the tens of thousands of Mayan farmers killed by the army. Spain, a country sympathetic to the plight of indigenous Guatemalans, agreed to investigate the genocide carried on by former Guatemalan presidents. Finally on May 10, 2013, a three-judge panel of the Guatemalan courts sentenced former dictator Ríos Montt to an 80-year jail term for genocide and crimes against humanity. Rigoberta felt vindicated, saying, "We need justice for the victims for there to be real peace." Her sense of victory was short lived—the high court of Guatemala overturned his conviction less than two weeks later.

Rigoberta still had much work to do, bringing real peace to her country and to the planet. Along with 12 other Nobel Peace laureates, five of them women, Rigoberta participates in Peace Jam, a program to teach youth the art of peace. Her message is simple: during dark times we need to increase the light.

"To be a light to others you will need a good dose of the spiritual life," says Rigoberta. "Because as my mother used to say, if you are in a good place, then you can help others; but if you're not well, then go look for somebody who is in a good place who can help you."

KALPONA AKTER

---◆---

Garment Workers in Solidarity

"If they had let me keep my job, I would just be a problem-maker in a single factory. Instead I'm a problem-maker in the entire industry." —Kalpona Akter

---

Stepping cautiously through the concrete rubble of a collapsed building, Kalpona Akter carefully scanned the debris for evidence. She had just arrived home in Dhaka, Bangladesh, from a tour in the United States to raise awareness about the hazards facing her nation's garment workers. While there, she had received word of the collapse of an eight-story building where hundreds of workers sewed clothing in five factories located there.

As she got reports from friends, Kalpona was saddened to hear the number of deaths grow from an initial estimate of 40 to a final tally of 1,129. Of the 2,515 workers injured, some suffered severe wounds that prevented them from ever doing factory work again. This was the worst disaster in the history of

Kalpona Akter at Rana Plaza collapse site.
Bangladesh Center for Workers Solidarity

the garment industry, far worse than New York City's historic Triangle Shirtwaist Factory fire in 1911 that killed 145 workers.

Kalpona and others found labels for numerous clothing brands being made in the factories including those for Primark, Benetton, the Children's Place, and Joe Fresh. Kalpona told a reporter, "American companies know this is happening. We've told them, 'Remember these human faces. You killed these girls.'"

————

Born in 1977, Kalpona Akter was her parents' first child. Her father was a construction contractor in Dhaka, the biggest city in Bangladesh. Bordering India and Burma, Bangladesh is the most densely populated country in the world. It is only three times the size of New York State but is home to half as many people as reside in the entire United States. Kalpona grew up amid the hustle and bustle of a typical Dhaka neighborhood, where the calls of gregarious mynah and noisy bulbul birds blended with the urban racket of car horns and street vendors. Towering above apartments, houses, and shops were garment factories that employed many of Kalpona's neighbors. She attended the local school until her father became paralyzed from a stroke when she was 12 years old. As the eldest child, Kalpona became a breadwinner for the family that now included three younger sisters and a brother. Instead of strolling to class with her schoolmates, she joined the crowds of mostly women workers walking to a garment factory dressed in bright saris and *salwar kameezes*—traditional tunics, baggy pants, and headscarves.

For a short time Kalpona's mother also worked at a factory, but she had to quit to care for her baby daughter. Though only 10 years old, Kalpona's brother now had to abandon school as well to join her at the factory. Starting with the task of cutting material for belt loops, Kalpona was soon promoted to the more dangerous occupation of assembling garments at a sewing machine. She had to stay alert every second of her shift, which sometimes lasted more than 17 hours. One short lapse into daydreaming could lead to accidentally piercing her fingers with the needle. Her back, shoulders, and feet hurt after many hours bent over her machine. Her lungs hurt from breathing dust-filled air. Years after working in the factory she would still suffer from back pain.

"I had never seen anything like it," Kalpona recalled later of her startling transition to factory work. "The supervisors yelling, all the people crowded together, the long hours. What even made it worse was that I could see the playground at my old school from the roof of my factory," she remembered.

Even more terrible was the pay. For toiling 400 hours a month, she earned a mere six dollars (less than two cents an hour). There were no safety standards or compensation for work-related injuries. On days when the factory owner demanded they work 21-hour shifts to meet a production deadline, Kalpona and her brother would sleep on the factory floor for a few hours before resuming work. Without a cafeteria to eat in or adequate bathrooms, they were not only sleep deprived but also hungry and dirty. One day her factory caught fire and many of her coworkers were hurt in the frantic stampede to exit.

By the time Kalpona turned 16, she and her coworkers wanted to see a change in their working conditions. After discovering the Solidarity Center, a global workers rights organization affiliated with the AFL-CIO (American Federation of Labor and Congress of Industrial Organizations), they learned that the factory owners were violating Bangladeshi worker protection laws as well as cheating them out of wages. This knowledge opened Kalpona's eyes. "I was born a second time," she reminisced. "Until then I thought the owners were kind people who gave us jobs."

Kalpona devoted herself to the task of unionizing her fellow workers. Not only was she fired for this effort, but also the factory owner sent her photo around to other factory owners identifying her as a troublemaker. Denied the opportunity to work at another factory, Kalpona began a career as a union organizer. The bright, motivated young woman rapidly taught herself English, labor law, and computer skills. She spent endless hours working at the Bangladesh Center for Worker Solidarity, helped unionize the majority of her ex-coworkers, and was elected president of the center while still a teen. From that time, year after year she pushed for better working conditions. She provided adult literacy classes, health care, and loans to help

SWEATSHOPS

The term *sweatshop* came to use in England in reference to crowded, dangerous workplaces where employees produced garments under the supervision of a boss called the "sweater." The ready-made clothes produced in sweatshops were cheaper than those made by individual tailors. The rural poor, moving to cities such as London, were desperate for work and thus willing to work for a pittance. The garment industry flourished in cities that had an influx of impoverished immigrants. Deaths due to accidents, fire, and poor sanitation became commonplace. Only after unions and reformers demanded an end to these inhumane working conditions were laws passed guaranteeing basic rights.

workers while they sought new occupations after being fired from their jobs for joining a union.

Garment making is the largest industry in Bangladesh, employing millions of workers, the majority of whom are young women from impoverished rural families. These women are some of the lowest-paid workers in the world. Kalpona had been one of them, and now she was fighting against the government, factory owners, and big business to improve the lives of others by campaigning for a living wage, workplace safety, and the right for workers to form unions.

In October 2009 Kalpona joined other Bangladeshi labor activists in urging the government to review pay for garment workers, who were still earning a pittance—as little as six cents an hour. They recommended raising the monthly wage to $71 (29 cents an hour). Even though the activists emphasized that the current minimum wage was not enough to pay for the needs of a single worker for half of a month, factory owners refused to pay any more than $36 a month (15 cents an hour). Addressing this issue, Pope Francis described the pay scale as "slave wages."

Labor leaders organized factory strikes, mass protests, and demonstrations. Workers blocked main highways and clashed with police. Violence erupted on both sides. By the end of June 2010, 20,000 workers had protested in Dhaka. On June 30, numerous children were caught up in police attacks on workers. After the protest made international news, the government announced that on the first of November it would raise the monthly wage to $43 a month (18 cents an hour), a fraction of what workers demanded.

Also following the protests, several factory owners, including a Walmart contractor, filed charges against Kalpona and her union coworkers, accusing them of arson and inciting worker riots. Next, thugs abducted, beat, and cruelly tortured Aminul Islam, one of Kalpona's most skilled organizers. Threatening to kill him and his family, the thugs demanded that he sign a document stating that Kalpona and other colleagues were guilty of criminal acts. He bravely refused and managed to escape. Worried about Aminul's safety, Kalpona asked if he wanted to quit, but he refused. Kalpona found him a safer place to continue his work, away from the eyes of their enemies.

Instead of agreeing to meet workers' demands for safer working conditions and a living wage, the government organized a special police force to spy on labor activists and halt protests. When Kalpona received word that she would soon be arrested, she went into hiding as she continued her work. Eventually the police caught up with her, shackled Kalpona and her colleague, Babul Akhter, and hauled them off to jail. Both were confined for 11 days in a tiny two-foot-by-five-foot cell and interrogated for hours every day. The police beat Babul. The pair was released on bail after a month, but they still faced charges for crimes punishable by life in prison or death.

Aminul Islam was kidnapped again in April 2012. This time he did not escape. After being brutally tortured, he was killed and left by the side of the road. Kalpona felt responsible for not being able to prevent his death, and she was determined to bring his murderers to justice. Knowing that her life was also in danger intensified her campaign to bring international pressure on the government to cease attacks on labor activists and to improve working conditions. It would take two horrific disasters, however, to focus the eye of the media on Bangladesh's death trap factories.

On November 26, 2012, Tazreen Fashion's factory went up in flames. With more than 200 workers injured and 117 dead, this was the worst factory fire in history. Despite warnings of unsafe conditions, the owners had chosen to ignore the report. The fire ignited on the ground floor and spread quickly as fabric caught fire. As the rooms filled with smoke, workers ran for the stairway only to find the exit doors locked. The building lacked fire escapes, so many workers, like Sumi Abedin, jumped out the windows. She doubted she would survive that fall, but she wanted her parents to be able to identify her body. If she remained inside, she reasoned, she would be burned beyond recognition. Miraculously Sumi survived her leap from the third story. Rescuers discovered her on the ground, unconscious and with a broken leg, arm, and ankle.

Some companies, such as Walmart, denied using the Tazreen Fashion factory for production of their clothes, but Kalpona's search through the debris revealed remnants of clothing with Walmart labels as well as those of other companies. In December the *New York Times* reported that Walmart allegedly led efforts to block a plan requiring apparel retailers to fund improvements to factory safety.

In April 2013 Sumi joined Kalpona on the 10-day Death Traps Tour in the United States to raise awareness about safety and labor rights issues in Bangladesh. In each city where they held events Sumi told her story of the fire. On April 26, 2013, at an event in

OUTSOURCING

The tragic Triangle factory fire in New York in 1911 set in motion a social reform movement that shifted the US apparel industry from one that relied on sweatshops to one with safer unionized workplaces paying middle-class wages. Clothes produced by union workers bore a "Union Made" label. By 2000 the garment industry declined in the United States as clothing retailers began outsourcing apparel production to nonunion factories in developing nations such as China and Bangladesh. By paying foreign workers wages just a fraction of those paid to workers in the United States, these companies were able to keep prices low.

Seattle, a reporter asked her if she would work at a garment factory again. Sumi replied, "I don't want to, I'm really afraid that if I get a job in another factory there will be a fire again."

That very night the Rana Plaza factory building, located in a Dhaka suburb, collapsed. More than 1,000 workers died. The previous day workers had reported seeing a large crack in a wall. Supervisors said that it was nothing to worry about. Those workers who risked their jobs by choosing to stay home the following day survived. Many of those who showed up for fear of being fired were injured or killed.

A tragedy of this size could not be ignored. In 2012 when US Secretary of State Hillary Clinton visited Bangladesh to meet with Prime Minister Sheikh Hasina, she expressed concerns about harassment of union organizers, and especially the murder of Aminul Islam. Concerned about treatment of union activists and factory safety, the United States suspended a favorable trade agreement with Bangladesh in June 2013. Good news came in July when the Bangladeshi government dropped charges against Babul and Kalpona. The authorities also promised the search for Aminul Islam's murderers would be reinvigorated.

Help also came from the Model Alliance, an organization of professional models, ex-models, and others urging the fashion industry to address issues such as child labor, workers' rights, eating disorders, and sexual abuse in the fashion workplace. They and other US labor rights groups joined Kalpona in urging US brands to sign the safety accord. By October 2013 more than 100 companies had signed the accord ensuring that one-third of the Bangladeshi garment factories would receive funds to maintain safe buildings. But some giant enterprises such as Walmart, Gap, and Sears refused to sign the accord.

In December 2013 the owners of the Tazreen Factory were charged with homicide, but Kalpona had much more work to do, especially convincing big retailers to sign the safety accord. Speaking at a Walmart board meeting she said, "I am sure you are aware that fixing these buildings would cost just a tiny fraction of your family's wealth, so I implore you to please help us. You have the power to do this very easily. Don't you agree that the factories where Walmart products are made should be safe for the workers?"

Speaking in English before a group of the rich and powerful had become routine for Kalpona. For someone who had to drop out of school to toil in a factory, this was quite a remarkable journey, one that she won't abandon until workers triumph.

PART III

REJECTING VIOLENCE

JANE ADDAMS

———◆———

Weaving the Safety Net,
Joining Hands for Peace

"The public and government have a duty toward the weak and defenseless members of society." —Jane Addams

---

I n London, England, 23-year-old Jane Addams witnessed a scene of despair much like those in the novels she had read by Charles Dickens. Before her were starving men, women, and children in ragged, unwashed clothes, desperately trying to get their hands on food so spoiled no one else wanted it. Foul odors and heartrending pleas for food filled the air.

This was a world Jane had never witnessed before, and it greatly disturbed her. She felt useless and was horrified that she was not expected to do anything in the face of such pain and suffering. Always sensitive to the needs of others, Jane now faced her future.

═══════

Jane Addams was born
on September 6, 1860,
five months after the
start of the Civil War, in
Cedarville, Illinois. She
was Sarah and John Huy
Addams's eighth child.
John was a successful
businessman and a state
senator. Sarah was well
respected for her kind-
ness to neighbors.

The Addams lived a comfortable life, but not one without
tragedy. Three of the Addams children had died in infancy.
Within two years of the third death, Sarah was pregnant again.
One icy, wintry night she slipped and fell. She lost her baby and
died a few days later. It was a wrenching loss. Jane, still a tod-
dler, was now cared for by her older sister Martha. A year later
young Jane contracted spinal tuberculosis, leaving her with a
crooked back and a limp. When Jane was six Martha died suddenly from typhoid fever. Rather than making her bitter, these
hardships gave Jane compassion. As if seeing into the future, she
told her father that she wished to live next to poor families so
she could help them.

Despite her limp Jane was a daring risk taker—sometimes
foolishly so. At her father's sawmill, without his knowledge, she
would sit on a log as it slowly advanced toward the great circular

saw blade and then leap off just in time to avoid being sliced in two—an extremely dangerous thing to do!

Jane was eight when her father married Anna Hostetter Haldeman, a widow with two sons. Jane's older sisters had grown and gone, and Jane was happy to have another female in the house, especially one who shared her interests in reading, conversation, fashion, and travel.

Jane's father, however, would always remain the center of her life. He arose at 4 AM each morning, a habit from his days as a miller. Like him, Jane awoke early with the goal of reading her way through each book in his library. Among the books she was fascinated with was Thomas Carlyle's *On Heroes, Hero-Worship, and the Heroic in History*. Knowing that her father had opposed slavery and risked his freedom and career to help escaped slaves travel to Canada on the Underground Railroad made him her personal hero. Jane loved eavesdropping on his conversations with visiting politicians, and she treasured a letter written to her father by his friend President Abraham Lincoln that began with "My dear Double-D-'ed Addams." John Addams was Christian, but he refused to align with any particular church and taught Jane to "always be honest with yourself inside, whatever happened."

Jane dreamed of being a doctor so she could help the needy. She was eager to attend the newly opened Smith College for women in Massachusetts to accomplish her goal, but she yielded to the wishes of her father. He wanted her to study at Rockford Female Seminary because it was nearby. Jane was deeply disappointed. Not only did Rockford not award bachelor's degrees like Smith did, but it emphasized a fundamentalist Christian faith, with daily sermons, rote memorization of bible passages, and insistence that students "come to Jesus" through baptism. Like her father, Jane was determined to resist aligning with a particular brand of Christianity.

"I felt that this passive resistance of mine, this clinging to an individual conviction, was the best moral training I received at Rockford College," she later said.

Fortunately for Jane she found a mentor in Caroline Potter, a professor thrilled by the growing women's rights movements. Under Potter's influence Jane thrived. She wrote editorials for the school magazine, gave speeches at the college, and eventually competed as the only female student at an intercollegiate oratorical contest at a men's college. In 1881 Jane graduated at the top of her class, ready to practice the power of her convictions as Potter had taught—but that meant going head-to-head with her strong-willed father. As she feared, he continued to deny her wish to study at Smith College.

In the immediate future one circumstance after another would prevent Jane from pursuing her ambitions. The summer following her graduation, her father died unexpectedly from appendicitis. He had been the one constant in her life, her anchor. Now without either parent Jane sank into a depression.

Once she had been ready to take on the world, but Jane now found her path blocked. It took eight years for her to redirect her life. In the fall of 1881 she moved with her stepmother to Philadelphia. Pursuing her dream to help the less fortunate, both she and her sister Alice enrolled in the Woman's Medical College of Philadelphia. But Jane was forced to abandon her studies after only one year as her health deteriorated. After undergoing surgery to straighten her back, Jane suffered a nervous breakdown. Her doctor recommended travel to speed along her recovery, so in 1883 she and her stepmother set off on a two-year tour of Europe. In London Jane had the experience in the slums that would set her back on course.

Back in the United States, feeling trapped in the life of an unmarried young woman without a career, Jane immersed herself in books. An article about Toynbee Hall in London caught Jane's attention. Called a settlement house, the hall was a daring experiment to address the needs of the poor. A couple months later, in December 1887, she embarked for Europe with her college friend Sarah Anderson. There they joined Jane's best friend from college, Ellen Gates Starr. While Ellen and Sarah were off on side travels, Jane visited Toynbee Hall. It was a life-changing event. In a letter to her sister Alice, Jane wrote, "It is so free of 'professional doing good,' so unaffectedly sincere and

SETTLEMENT HOUSES

In the 19th century there was very little assistance for the poor. No food stamps, welfare, or medical care. Toynbee Hall was a place where educated young men, called residents, could live and work as volunteers in London's East End. By facing poverty on a daily basis and developing relationships with their neighbors they hoped to discover practical solutions to real problems. At the hall working people and residents could mingle as equals and share ideas. Residents could share their education in the arts, literature, and history through free classes. Charity toward the sick and elderly, and coming to aid in emergencies, would be accomplished as neighbors caring for neighbors. The Hall, as the first settlement house, was a place where working people could learn the skills to prosper in mind and body.

so productive of good results in all its classes and libraries that it seems perfectly ideal."

Since childhood Jane had desired to live among the poor. Now she saw the way. She shared her dream of opening a settlement house in the United States with Ellen, who was so enthusiastic she offered to help. Since Ellen lived in Chicago, where she worked as a schoolteacher, they decided to establish it there. With amazing luck Jane found a large house built nearly 35 years before by real estate magnate Charles Hull in an area that was at that time outside the city. Now it was surrounded by the city in a neighborhood called the 19th Ward that was jam-packed with Italian, German, Irish, Bohemian, and Jewish immigrants. The house, which had served as a factory, store, and a home for the aged, was badly in need of repairs. Jane paid for these, as well as the rent, with money from the large inheritance from her father. Calling it Hull House, they had no notion it would one day be known worldwide.

The house was big and beautiful enough to suit Jane's dream. Neighborhood residents were reluctant to visit at first, but before long 2,000 visitors a week flocked to Hull House to make use of its services. These included adult night school, kindergarten, clubs for older children, a kitchen open to the public, an art gallery, a gym, a bathhouse, a bookbindery, a library, a coffeehouse, a music school, and a drama group. Over the years the settlement facility expanded to include 13 buildings, a playground, a summer camp, a labor museum, a club for single working girls, meeting rooms for unions, and performance space for an array of cultural events.

At first the funds mostly came from Jane, but donations eventually poured in. The landlord soon offered the property rent-free. All activities were guided by Ellen and Jane's three main ethical principles: teach by example, cooperate, and demonstrate social democracy. With the talents and energy of residents, Hull House addressed one social issue after another. Studies of everything from typhoid fever and truancy to overcrowding, infant mortality, drug use, and midwifery were conducted. Hull House research and programs addressing the needs of neighborhood residents grew into city- and statewide campaigns to improve housing, improve child labor laws and schools, establish playgrounds, and guarantee protection for working women. Jane herself investigated narcotics, milk supplies, and neighborhood sanitation problems and how they affected people's health. With typical zeal she even accepted the post of official garbage inspector for the 19th Ward.

By 1893, 19 settlement houses had been established in the United States. Among these, Hull House was the largest and best known. During the Chicago World's Fair, visitors from around the nation and world came to learn about Jane Addams and Hull House. As rewarding as this attention was, Jane was struggling with how to serve residents of the 19th Ward who had lost jobs and in many cases their homes during the financial crisis of that year. As she witnessed people trying to feed themselves and their families, Jane realized that libraries, art galleries, classes, and gymnasiums were not enough. Hull House opened a free health clinic and a relief bureau to connect people in need with charities that could help them. Unable to convince her fellow residents to open a homeless shelter, she worked with women's clubs in Chicago to find shelter for families in need.

Through her articles, books, and hundreds of speeches she gave throughout the country Jane became a major advocate for addressing social ills. In 1908 *Ladies' Home Journal* called Jane the "Foremost American Woman." In 1910 Yale University bestowed Jane with an honorary degree, its first ever given to a woman. Smith College, where Jane long ago dreamed of

HULL HOUSE RESIDENTS

Among the women residents at Hull House were those who later took on major roles in promoting social change. Julia Lathrop, known as "America's First Official Mother," pushed for laws to protect children and was appointed the first director of the new Children's Bureau in 1912. Florence Kelley became the chief factory inspector of Illinois, founded the National Consumers League, and fought for safe working conditions. She organized a boycott of clothes made by nonunion workers and, along with Jane Addams, helped establish the National Association for the Advancement of Colored People (NAACP). Dr. Alice Hamilton, an expert in industrial health (occupational health), studied workplace accidents and illness and lobbied for healthy work conditions in factories and mills.

attending, awarded her one as well. Jane also served on an advisory board for the newly formed Campfire Girls, the first nonsectarian, interracial US organization for girls. From 1911 to 1914 Jane served as vice president of the National Woman Suffrage Association.

By the second decade of the 20th century, Jane's diverging causes for peace, suffrage, equality for African Americans, and social justice were coming together under the banner of humanitarianism. She envisioned a world where the "great reservoirs of human ability" would be honored. Soldiers from poor families wouldn't be wasted as cannon fodder, women would have an equal voice and the choice to pursue their paths, and children who were free from laboring in factories and mines could reach their potential.

After the start of World War I in 1914, Jane stepped up her involvement in the growing peace movement. The following year she was chosen as chair for the Women's Peace Party and then became president of the new Women's International League for Peace and Freedom. Both organizations opposed the entry of the United States in the war. The organizations campaigned for President Woodrow Wilson and leaders of other neutral nations to work together in negotiating peace between the warring factions. Jane had been born during one of the most horrific wars of the 19th century; now she tried her best to end another.

When Congress voted to join England and France in fighting Germany, politicians and journalists viciously attacked dissenters, like Jane Addams. She received hate letters and was booed when she gave speeches. Despite being shaken by the disregard of free speech during time of war, Jane stuck to her belief. After the armistice, Jane joined Herbert Hoover in providing food to the women and children in the defeated nations. In 1920 she joined fellow suffragist and peace activist Crystal Eastman as one of the founders of the American Civil Liberties Union.

For someone who had poor health in her early years, she had pursed her life's mission with phenomenal energy. Following a heart attack in 1926, Jane never regained her vigor. She resigned her presidency of the Women's International League for Peace and Freedom and was appointed honorary president for life. On December 10, 1931, Jane learned that she had won

Jane Addams, 1928.
Swarthmore College Peace Collection

the Nobel Peace Prize, the first American woman to be so honored. Throughout her life until her death on May 21, 1935, Jane had great hope for diminishing the social ills plaguing humanity. In her 74 years she did more than most through education and advocacy to make the world a better place.

IDA B. WELLS

---◆---

Shining the Light on Lynching

"I'd rather go down in history as one lone Negro who dared to tell the government that it had done a dastardly thing than to save my skin by taking back what I said." —Ida B. Wells

---

Day after day Ida Wells, a 21-year-old schoolteacher, purchased a first-class train ticket, sat down in the first-class ladies coach, and rode to the town outside Memphis where she taught. Then one day in May 1884, out of the blue, a conductor refused to accept her ticket and rudely ordered her to sit in the smoker car reserved for blacks.

Raised to demand respect, Ida refused to budge. The conductor and two baggage men physically overpowered her and dragged Ida, biting and kicking, off the train. Ida was enraged by this abuse of her rights and filed a lawsuit against the railroad, arguing it had violated the Civil Rights Act of 1866. The local court ruled in her favor and awarded her $500 in damages. A year later the Tennessee Supreme Court reversed the decision.

Ida B. Wells, 1893.
Wikimedia Commons

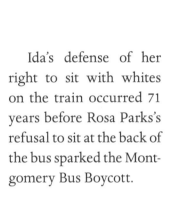

Ida's defense of her right to sit with whites on the train occurred 71 years before Rosa Parks's refusal to sit at the back of the bus sparked the Montgomery Bus Boycott.

—————

Ida Bell Wells was born into slavery on July 16, 1862, in Holly Springs, Mississippi, to her enslaved parents, James Wells and Elizabeth "Lizzie Bell" Warrenton. Only six months later President Abraham Lincoln signed the Emancipation Proclamation setting slaves free. Her parents' days of slavery were over.

James's father was a white plantation owner who had started a black "family" with his slave Peggy when his wife failed to bear children. He apprenticed James at the age of 18 to a carpenter, Spires Bolling. This training guaranteed James a better life than that of a field slave, and it was at the Bolling home where James fell in love with Lizzie Bell, one of their kitchen slaves. Ida was the first of their eight children.

After the war James agreed to work for Spires Bolling. When James actively supported African American candidates seeking office as Republicans, Spires was enraged. Like many other white townspeople, Spires hoped to prevent political change by coercing black townspeople to vote for white candidates. In retaliation for James's voting as he wished, Spires locked James out of the carpentry workshop.

Without a word to his former employer, James purchased tools for his own business, rented a house, and moved his family from Spires's premises. James Wells's actions, more than his words, primed Ida for life as a crusader. Lizzie Wells influenced Ida as well with her strict discipline and expectation that her children be responsible to both family and community.

Masters had kept their slaves illiterate with the intent of keeping them ignorant. With the help of the Freedman's Aid Society and teachers from the North, schools such as Shaw University were established to provide African American children with an education. The young white female teachers who taught Ida provided her with role models of independent, outspoken, and gracious women. Ida's sense of righteousness and her willingness to speak her mind, qualities that would make her a leader in adulthood, caused trouble at school. A clash with the school president once led to her expulsion. Later in life Ida would learn to tame her bad temper without putting reins on her sense of right.

In 1878 a yellow fever epidemic killed more than 300 residents of Holly Springs, black and white. Ida's parents and her baby brother Stanley were among the dead. Ida, who had been staying at her grandmother's farm, returned home to care for her siblings. Friends of the family discussed splitting up the children and parceling them out to families willing to care for them. Though only 16 years old, Ida fiercely opposed the plan, assuring the friends that she could take care of them on her own, with the help of Grandmother Peggy.

When the family savings were used up Ida took a job as a teacher. In 1883, when her brothers were old enough to be on their own, she moved with her two youngest sisters to Memphis, Tennessee, to live with her widowed Aunt Fannie and her three small children. Ida found a teaching job outside Memphis. It was during this time that she resisted being forced out of her first-class seat on the train. During summers she took classes at Fisk University in Nashville.

Ida was energetic and ambitious. She changed jobs to a school in the city of Memphis with 650 black students and only nine teachers. Now with less time spent commuting to work, she began writing for a Baptist journal, *The Living Way*. Her column often highlighted racial injustices, and soon other African

RECONSTRUCTION

In 1863 President Lincoln declared Southern slaves free; in 1866 the 13th Amendment brought an end to slavery in the entire United States. In 1870 the 15th Amendment gave black men the right to vote. African Americans could vote, be elected to political office, purchase land, start their own businesses, and use public accommodations. In 1872 Louisiana people elected a black governor, and by 1878 whites were the minority in the South Carolina legislature. Yet over time, state laws were enacted that institutionalized discrimination and segregation, and suppressed the voting of black citizens.

American publications asked her to write. Within five years she was elected secretary of the Afro-American Press Association and nicknamed the "Princess of the Press." Ida became an editor in 1889 when she bought a one-third interest in Memphis's *The Free Speech and Headlight*. She now she had a platform to express her opinions to Memphis's black community.

As in most of the South, schools in Memphis were segregated. Ida decried the inferior condition of black students' school buildings and the "poor teachers whose mental and moral quality was not the best." Incensed, the school administration declined to rehire her. She now became a full-time journalist, and before long her activism in the wake of a tragic incident would incite the wrath of white supremacists.

When three African American men, Tom Moss, Calvin McDowell, and Will Stewart, opened the Peoples Grocery Store in their black neighborhood, residents flocked to it. The other neighborhood market, owned by a white man, lost business as a result. If the new grocery had been owned by white people, it would have been seen as normal competition, but competition from a black-owned business was seen as a declaration of war.

On the night of March 9, 1891, supporters of the white grocer attacked the Peoples Grocery Store. Some of the attackers were shot in the scuffle as Moss, McDowell, and Stewart defended their business. The attackers were not arrested, but Moss, McDowell, and Stewart were hauled off to jail. It wasn't long before a white mob dragged them out and shot them. Their deaths shocked the black community. The victims were well-loved men who had provided a service to their neighborhood.

Ida had been away from Memphis during the murders. Upon hearing the news she was outraged and, after her return, declared war against vigilante justice, or lynching. Ida traveled around the South gathering information on lynchings in other towns.

She wrote, "There is therefore only one thing left that we can do; save our money and leave a town which will neither protect our lives and property, nor give us a fair trial in the courts, but takes us out and murders us in cold blood when accused by white persons." People followed her advice. The departure of more than 6,000 African Americans meant loss of customers and laborers to white enterprises.

Her articles angered the white community, but Ida was fearless. Friends warned her that she was putting her life in danger, so she armed herself with a pistol and plunged ahead. In a subsequent article she declared, "Nobody in this section of the country believes the old thread-bare lie that Negro men rape white women. If Southern white men are not careful, they will overreach themselves and public sentiment will have a reaction; a conclusion will then be reached which will be very damaging to the moral reputation of their women."

Ida's implication that white women willfully had romantic relationships with black men unleashed the fury of racist white men. While she was away, a white mob destroyed her printing equipment, wrecked her office, and drove her business manager out of town. A note left behind warned, "Anyone attempting to publish the paper again will be punished with death."

The threat only strengthened Ida's resolve to stop lynching. She accepted the offer to write for and become a business partner of the *New York Age*, a widely distributed black newspaper. Rather than silencing Ida, the thugs in Memphis had given her an opportunity to tell the truth about lynching to an even larger audience.

In New York, Ida published a pamphlet, *Southern Horrors: Lynch Laws in All Its Phases*, highlighting results of her investigation of lynching and demonstrating how lynching was used to terrorize blacks to insure white supremacy. Ida became the voice of the antilynching campaign, both in print and on the

LYNCHING

Lynching is an execution of individuals by a mob. In the United States between the 1830s and 1860s most victims were white. From the 1860s on, black people, primarily in the South, were targeted. Victims were accused, often falsely, of crimes such as rape, murder, and robbery—or even minor offenses such as trying to register to vote, testifying against or insulting a white man, and even asking a white woman to marry. Railroads offered excursions to lynchings, where photographs were taken, and whites gathered as if at a jubilee while watching victims being tortured before being killed. Postcards of lynchings were sold and mailed by spectators to friends. Both men and women were lynched, some as young as 14. Between the 1880s and 1920s at least 1,000 African Americans died from lynching.

podium. She was invited to give speeches, often to large groups, organized by prominent black women.

Worried that she would seem unprofessional if she became teary-eyed as she talked of the lynching in Memphis, Ida discovered that her emotion only emphasized the gravity of her message. Invitations to give speeches came from cities throughout the East Coast. At each event people donated funds to her cause, and she met prominent members of the American black community such as Frederick Douglass.

In the spring of 1893 Ida accepted an invitation to give lectures in England and Scotland. Her talks received widespread attention in the press. She made friends with editors of prominent newspapers and leading clergymen, and she stayed with well-known women suffragists and writers such as Isabella Fyvie Mayo. Her tour led to the formation of the British Anti-Lynching League; members included the archbishop of Canterbury, members of Parliament, a Scottish duke, and the editors of the *Manchester Guardian*.

Back in the United States, Ida moved to Chicago where, at the age of 33, she married Ferdinand Barnett, a lawyer and owner of the *Conservator*, Chicago's first black newspaper. Born in Tennessee, Ferdinand had earned his law degree in Chicago. His first wife had died, leaving him with two sons. The marriage of Ida and Ferdinand became a partnership not only of love and family but also of dedication to social justice. Ferdinand respected Ida for her work, and he sold the *Conservator* to her so she would have her own journal to protest injustice.

Soon Ida was pregnant with their first child. "My duties as editor, as president of the Ida B. Wells Woman's Club, and as a speaker at many white women's clubs around Chicago kept me pretty busy," wrote Ida. "But I was not too busy to find time to give birth to a male child the following 25 March 1896." Since Ida was nursing baby Charles, she took him along on speaking tours. At each event, whether sponsored by white or black groups, a nurse was provided to hold Charles while Ida gave her speech.

By 1904 Ida had given birth to three more children: Herman, Ida Jr., and Alfreda. Ida was torn between the joys and obligations of mothering and commitment to her work. After Herman's birth she took a break from touring to devote herself to her family. In 1901 Ida and Ferdinand bought a home (later designated as a historic landmark) in an all-white neighborhood, but she did not abandon her people.

In September 1909, she and Ferdinand learned of the lynching in Cairo, Illinois, of a black man, Will "Frog" James, who was accused of murdering a white woman. Before he could be tried and found innocent or guilty, a white mob dragged him to the main square where a large crowd watched him die by hanging. The lynching was a horrid travesty, and it occurred in their home state of Illinois. The previous year a new state law had passed requiring the dismissal of any sheriff who failed to adequately protect a prisoner from a lynch mob. Cairo's sheriff, Frank Davis, was fired for not protecting Will James. Now he and his supporters were asking the governor to return him to his job.

Not a single black leader in Chicago planned to argue against the reinstatement of the sheriff, so Ida traveled to Cairo. There she gathered the testimony of black residents and convinced a majority of them to sign a statement confirming the sheriff's inaction. She then went on to the state capital, Springfield, where she was the sole African American and lone protester presenting a case against the sheriff. Her thorough evidence made it impossible for the governor to ignore the sheriff's dereliction of duty. By forcing the governor to uphold the law, Ida sent a strong warning to other racist sheriffs in the state. Thus she effectively put an end to lynching in Illinois.

In the following years Ida founded the National Afro-American Council and the Women's Era Club, the first civic organization for African American women. When a prominent white minister stated that even though the black community was only 3 percent of Chicago's population it accounted for 10 percent of the crimes, Ida responded, saying that settlement houses and organizations such as the YMCA that supported newcomers to the city refused to serve African Americans and that "only one social center welcomes the Negro, and that is the saloon." Segregation was still the norm, and even reformers like Jane Addams weren't willing to rock the boat by integrating settlement houses like Hull House.

With financial help from the owner of the *Daily News* she and others opened the Negro Fellowship League Reading Room and Social Center in May 1910. Within a short time they added a small men's lodging house upstairs. By the end of the year 40 to 50 men were using the center each day, and 115 men had found jobs with the center's help.

Ida continued to be so outspoken that she and Ferdinand, who assisted with legal issues, were sometimes labeled as being too militant. Ida seldom held back when she had something to say. She had become a close friend of Susan B. Anthony, a crusader for women's right to vote. Though she greatly admired Anthony, 40 years her senior, Ida criticized her for not working with Southern black suffragists due to fear of losing the backing of Southern white supporters.

On at least one occasion Ida caught the attention of government officials. In April 1917 black soldiers stationed outside of Houston rioted after two of their comrades were beaten and jailed by police for no other reason except inquiring about the arrest of a black woman. Nineteen soldiers were hanged and 41 were given life sentences. During this time of war any criticisms of the government were regarded as treason. Ida had buttons printed to pass out at a memorial service she hoped to arrange for the executed soldiers, but not one of the black churches in Chicago would host the memorial. After Ida started selling the buttons to anyone wanting to protest the deaths, Secret Service agents showed up at her door threatening to jail her. Ida responded that it would be an honor to be arrested for criticizing her government when she felt it was wrong. Cowed by her courage, they let her be.

Ida was working on her autobiography when she died of kidney disease on March 25, 1931, just short of her 70th birthday. Having been freed from slavery, Ida fought against the continued denial of rights and freedoms. Though small in stature she made her voice heard in defense of black people. Whether they admired or reviled her, people listened to what Ida B. Wells had to say as she set the stage for the civil rights movement of the 1960s.

BUFFY SAINTE-MARIE

---◆---

It Shines Through Her

"I sang 'Now That the Buffalo Is Gone' until I was sick of people coming to see the little Indian girl cry. But nothing happened, did it? The change is going to have to come from within us, the Indian people." –Buffy Sainte-Marie

---

The audience erupted in applause following Buffy Sainte-Marie's performance of her song "Now That the Buffalo's Gone." This powerful lament about the theft of Indian lands and "My Country 'Tis of Thy People You're Dying," a startling ballad about the genocide and negative propaganda against Native Americans, were just right for this particular event. As one of the country's most prominent Native American performers and songwriters Buffy was helping young activists in the budding American Indian Movement who were boldly occupying Alcatraz Island in San Francisco Bay that December of 1969.

A month earlier, activists had publicly claimed that ownership of the island should revert to local Native Americans.
Supporting their argument was a clause in an 1868 treaty that
stated federal land no longer used by the government should be
returned to American Indians. The island housed the infamous
Alcatraz Federal Penitentiary, which had closed in 1963. Under
the cover of darkness the activists, mostly students, occupied
Alcatraz. Within days more Indian activists joined them and
their act of defiance became national and international news.
Buffy was doing her part to raise money for supplies and to rally
the public to support the cause.

———

Buffy Sainte-Marie's beginnings are shrouded in mystery. She
was told her birthplace was Craven, a village near the Piapot
Cree Reserve on the plains of Saskatchewan, Canada, but she
never saw a birth certificate documenting her birth. She was
told her mother and father were Cree, but she never knew their
names or why they gave her up for adoption. She knew that she
was born in February 1941, possibly on the 20th, but she never
knew if her birth parents gave her a name.

She did know that Albert and Winifred Sainte-Marie adopted
her and named her Beverly Jean. Winifred had Micmac Indian
ancestors in Nova Scotia and told little Beverly of her Cree ances-
try. The Sainte-Maries had welcomed her into their family when
their oldest child, Alan, was five years old and shortly after the
death of their second son, Wayne, at four months of age.

The Sainte-Maries were considered poor, and their home in
Wakefield, Massachusetts, near Lake Quannapowitt was small
compared to the larger homes of their neighbors. Behind the
house were woods where Beverly (later called Buffy) connected

with the natural world. Inside the house was a piano, which led her into the world of music. From a young age Buffy heard music in her mind. By playing with the piano as a toy Buffy quickly taught herself to play, and she created her own compositions before she was old enough to go to school.

Winifred was a loving mother, a safe island in a sea of hostility and confusion.

"I was raised in a situation where certain family members didn't welcome me and others did. There were pedophiles in the neighborhood, the family, and in the house," said Buffy in an interview. Buffy looked different than her family members and did not like the fact that she was adopted. She was bullied and harassed by neighborhood children, but she realized what set her apart was not her physical appearance but her artistic temperament. She was a creative soul, an artist and musician living in a community where her talents were not valued. Even the music and art taught in school didn't seem to reflect the blazing creativity that burned inside her. Aware of her Indian heritage, Buffy felt invisible.

"It wasn't possible to be an Indian in my town. I lived in New England, where people didn't believe in Indians. They thought the Indians were all dead and stuffed in museums like wolves and eagles," commented Buffy. As Buffy grew older her cultural identity was strengthened by her friendship with a Narragansett Indian family who lived within bicycling distance on the other side of the lake.

At age 16, Buffy taught herself how to play guitar. During summer vacations along the shores of Lake Sebago, Maine, she spent hours outdoors composing and singing her own songs. In the fall of 1959 she entered the University of Massachusetts, Amherst. For the first time Buffy saw herself as smart. She became passionate about learning, and she enjoyed exploring new subjects, especially world religions. Courses that addressed the true history of American Indians confirmed Winifred's insight that "the Indians did not lose to the white people because of fair fights and majority odds and superior weaponry," but because "Indians have been cheated and cheated and cheated again and still are cheated and cheated again."

Buffy had described her painfully shy high school persona as "Mrs. Mouse." But, in college she burst out of her shell as she made friends with fellow students. A housemother at her dorm encouraged Buffy to perform and work harder at songwriting. She jammed with other students, including Henry Fredericks, a musician of Native American and African American heritage. Like Buffy, he would also achieve fame as a musician under the name Taj Mahal.

Buffy gained more fans as she composed and performed new protest and love songs. Her special talent earned recognition. She was voted one of the 10 most outstanding U-Mass graduates of 1962. Now "Mrs. Mouse" was ready to explore the world.

With money earned from coffeehouse performances, Buffy set off on a journey to explore her roots. At a powwow on Manitoulin Island in Lake Ontario she met Emile Piapot, the last surviving son of Chief Piapot, the famed leader of the Plains Cree. Emile was traveling with other Cree singers and dancers from the Piapot Reserve. Buffy told him about her origins, and Emile revealed that he had once given up a baby daughter for adoption. Feeling a special connection Emile invited her to visit his family. Later that year when Buffy visited the reserve, the family warmly accepted her as one of their own. Buffy was truly at home, learning the ways of the elders, appreciating the gifts of the creator, and basking in the wisdom of her rediscovered community.

"In my own language [Cree] there is no word for art," Buffy once explained, saying that instead the Cree say, "It shines

Buffy Sainte-Marie at Peterborough Summer Festival of Lights,
June 24, 2009.
Monica Vereana Williams

through him," meaning that the artist is a medium for the creator.

In the early 1960s New York City's Greenwich Village became the epicenter for folk music. When Buffy arrived there in 1963 she quickly gained notice. Her songs spoke of contemporary issues. At one of her first performances, a 22-year-old musician named Bob Dylan praised her act. At his recommendation she performed at another coffeehouse, the Gaslight, where many folk musicians and comedians launched their careers during the 1960s. A prominent music critic caught her act, penned an enthusiastic review, and helped connect her with Vanguard Records. Her first album, *It's My Way*, made waves in the music world. The words of her antiwar song "The Universal Soldier" spoke to everyone's responsibility for war.

> *And he knows he shouldn't kill, And he knows he always will*
> *Kill you for me my friend and me for you.*

Her song "Cod'ine," inspired by Buffy getting hooked on codeine in a cough medicine prescribed by a doctor, graphically portrayed drug addiction.

> *If I lived till tomorrow it's gonna be a long time*
> *For I'll reel and I'll fall and rise on codine*

Buffy rocketed into fame. *Billboard* magazine named her the Best New Artist of 1964. Donovan's cover of "Universal Soldier" became a bestselling single. In recording her song "Now That the Buffalo's Gone," a plea to end the continued confiscation of Indian lands, she joined her new friend, musician Peter La Farge, in tackling a topic new to folk music. *It's My Way* was called one of the "most scathing topical folk albums ever made."

THE VIETNAM WAR PROTEST MOVEMENT

In the early 1960s the war in Vietnam expanded. As more and more young men were drafted, opposition to the war grew. By 1965 protestors staged large demonstrations against the war on both the East and West Coasts. Public sentiment against the war increased, eventually causing President Lyndon Johnson's decision not to seek reelection. Songs by musicians such as Buffy Sainte-Marie, Richie Havens, Bob Dylan, and Country Joe became anthems for the antiwar movement.

A person who had grown up in the shadows, Buffy was now in the spotlight. One critic wrote, "There is a sense of royalty about her, like royalty from a very funky, primitive planet somewhere. . . . When Buffy St. Marie enters a room everybody feels it."

All this fame and fortune came so quickly that Buffy had no time to learn about the business side of music. She naively accepted a stranger's assistance in establishing legal ownership for "Universal Soldier," only to discover later that she had been tricked into signing it over to him. Luckily her love song "Until It's Time You Go," which appeared on her next album, was recorded by so many other singers, from Elvis Presley to Cher and Willie Nelson, that it would provide Buffy a constant source of income. Within two years of her debut in the Village she had performed at London's Royal Albert Hall, in Australia, and in

Hong Kong. *Life* magazine reported she was earning $100,000 a year.

Needing a break from her grueling tour schedule she visited the Hawaiian isle of Kauai. She purchased a remote piece of property on the slope of a dormant volcano that would become her lifelong home. She took up surfing and fell in love with Dewain Kamaikalani Bugbee, a surfer with Hawaiian ancestors. Buffy married Dewain in 1968, at the age of 27. Together they worked their land in Kauai, planting acres of trees. They acquired a menagerie of horses, dogs, and goats. At first Dewain tried joining her on music tours, but he preferred to remain home. Buffy's life was mostly on the road, and the marriage didn't last.

In 1969 Buffy established a foundation to support the higher education of Native American youth, teaching them about their heritage and culture and the true history of Native Americans. She called it Nihewan, which means, "Talk Cree."

Meanwhile, unknown to Buffy, her music was being censored. Under orders from President Lyndon Johnson, radio stations were pressured not to play her music, especially "Universal Soldier." Her records were selling in Canada and Asia, but in the United States they were mysteriously absent from record stores. After Richard Nixon won the presidency, Buffy was added to his list of troublemakers as she continued to compose antiwar songs. Nixon did what he could to suppress Buffy's music. Almost 40 years later a covert CIA operative testified in court about the agency's campaign to silence music critical of government policies.

In 1975 Buffy married for the second time. Her Lakota husband, Sheldon Wolfchild, a Vietnam veteran and budding actor, was active in AIM (the American Indian Movement). Soon after their son Dakota (Cody) Starblanket Wolfchild was born, Buffy was asked to perform on *Sesame Street*. She agreed on the condition she could teach its young television audience that "Indians still exist." For the next five years children across the United States became familiar with Buffy as an American Indian woman who sang, told stories, counted with the Count in Cree, and even breast-fed and bathed her little baby Cody on air.

Through the 1960s and 1970s Buffy produced one album after another, a total of 16 by 1976. She then took a long break from her recording career to write musical scores for films, one of which, "Up Where We Belong," received an Academy Award for best song in 1982. Ten years later her next album featured yet more politically powerful songs such as "Bury My Heart at Wounded Knee."

We got the federal marshals, we got the covert spies . . .
They lie in court and get nailed and still Peltier goes off to jail

AMERICAN INDIAN MOVEMENT (AIM)

AIM began in Minneapolis to establish a patrol to defend urban Indians from police brutality, later adding health and legal rights centers to their programs. AIM activists staged occupations at Alcatraz Island, at a dam built on Ojibwa land, and in the town of Wounded Knee. During the latter conflict, AIM activist Leonard Peltier was convicted and sentenced to life imprisonment for killing two FBI agents in a trial that Amnesty International deemed unfair.

In 1996 Buffy launched the Cradleboard Teaching Project, now a web-based learning center providing public lessons about Native American culture, both in the past and present, as well as questions for the future.

In 2008 Buffy produced a hard-driving album, *Running for the Drum*, with danceable and powerful songs such as "No No Keshagesh." Meaning "greedy puppy" in Cree, "Keshagesh" compares greedy corporations stealing resources with a puppy that takes food from other puppies' bowls. At the age of 65 Buffy said, "It's futile to rush the river, and pretty hard to hurry the moon, and sometimes you have to be content to plant good seeds whenever you can and be patient as you watch them grow and ripen."

JUDY BACA

---◆---

Walls That Shout

"I was watching my cousins, my friends, in trouble, going to prison, drug abuse, and I thought, I can do something. I can help." —Judy Baca

---

During a period of unrest in the Mexican American neighborhood of East Los Angeles, Judy Baca began teaching art to young children and elderly women at local recreation centers. Just weeks before, on August 29, 1970, a riot had broken out when police attacked the peaceful National Chicano Moratorium March against the Vietnam War. One Chicano poet later said, "The police called it a people's riot: the people called it a police riot."

Judy felt most comfortable teaching teens. With her long, straight hair Judy looked like a teen herself. On her way to the rec centers she passed through a gauntlet of Chicano teens hanging out, drinking and doing drugs in the parks. Many were gang members. They made her coworkers nervous, but not Judy.

Judy Baca in front of *Great Wall* in Los Angeles.
SPARC

Each day she had a long break between morning and afternoon classes. Instead of going home she started hanging out
with the teens. She asked them about their graffiti and showed
them her paintings. "I started to become really good friends
with these guys—the so-called criminals, the element that was
considered to be the most feared," recalled Judy in an interview.

Judy's supervisors advised her not to encourage the teens to
hang around. The parks were gang territory. When Judy mentioned that she was getting them interested in painting murals,
her supervisors' attitude abruptly shifted. Judy had won the
teens' trust with her straight talk and belief that they were all
compadres, as part of *La Raza*, the Mexican race.

Many of the young people showed an interest in joining her on a project. When Judy discovered that a gang rehabilitation center had funds available to pay the youth, they jumped on board. Grandmothers are revered in Chicano families. So tough gang members or not, the young men liked the idea of painting a giant portrait of a smiling grandmother, *La Abuelita*, on the back wall of a park band shell. This was the start of Judy's lifework.

————

On September 26, 1946, Ortensia Baca gave birth to her daughter, Judith Francisca, at a home for unwed mothers in Huntington Park, near Los Angeles. The baby's father, a sailor who had a brief relationship with Ortensia, had moved on without knowing she was pregnant. Living with Judy and her mother in Watts were her two aunts and Grandmother Francisca, who cared for Judy while Ortensia worked in the Goodyear tire factory. Each day her mother came home smelling of rubber. Ortensia liked to draw. One of Judy's earliest memories was of the sketches her mother made to entertain her.

Grandmother Francisca taught Judy about her Mexican heritage and culture, especially the art of *curandismo*, folk healing. Francisca and her husband had fled Mexico after the Revolution of 1910, after banditos had confiscated their business. Cleverly Francisca had stashed their remaining money in a water pitcher, ensuring they had the funds to move across the border and on to Colorado.

With only Spanish being spoken at home, Judy struggled to communicate when she entered kindergarten in a school where languages other than English were forbidden. "I had an understanding of English but I didn't speak it so well, so my teacher set me up with a little easel and bright shiny tin cans of tempera paint. This wonderful teacher, whose name I can't remember, probably set the course of my life," recalled Judy. Little Judy loved painting and proudly brought her masterpieces home to her mother's delight.

When Judy was six, her mother married an Italian American named Clarence Ferrari. The family moved from predominately Mexican- and black-populated Watts to Pacoima, a suburb in the San Fernando Valley where there were few other people of color. Most of their neighbors, like her stepfather, worked for Lockheed Aircraft building planes. It was a different existence. Judy no longer lived with her grandmother and aunts. No longer could she speak Spanish at home. Her stepfather insisted on English only, and the same was true at school.

Judy's ability to express herself through art gave her an identity beyond being the "Mexican" girl at school. As her English improved so did her performance in other subjects. While attending Catholic high school Judy's reputation as an artist grew. "I would draw these little characters of naked screaming nuns running around the blackboard walls, and then I was, you know, punished regularly for that. But it amused everyone. . . . I would receive so much kind of reinforcement from my peers that I would endure the punishments of the nuns," recalled Judy.

Judy loved creating art, but she had never been to a museum or met an artist, and only knew of a few famous artists, Vincent Van Gogh being one. She knew nothing of the great artists of Mexico.

Judy was expected to become the first one in her family to attend college. Ortensia dreamed of Judy becoming a translator or, better yet, a lawyer. For Judy art always came first, and the only way her mother could see her having a career as an artist was to teach art. At California State University, Northridge, the worlds of philosophy, history, and sciences opened up to Judy. At 19 she impetuously married, but the marriage didn't last.

After graduating from college in 1969 Judy started teaching art at her old high school. She assembled a group of ethnically diverse students to work together painting a mural on a school wall. In this period of social upheaval tensions were strong. As Judy identified as a Chicana, an American woman of Mexican heritage, she began to question the dominant white dogma taught in the school. After Judy and other teachers publicly protested against the Vietnam War she and 16 of her colleagues were fired by the conservative school administration.

Judy then began teaching for the Los Angeles Department of Parks and Recreation, befriended the Chicano teens, and together with them painted *La Abuelita*, her first public mural.

"The police had been unfriendly to my efforts to bring known gang members into public sites. They said they would arrest my team members if I continued to assemble them in public view," Judy remembers.

The project got headlines in the press like, GANG MEMBERS PUT DOWN KNIVES FOR BRUSHES. The director of the park department, Sy Greben, came to see Judy at one of the parks. The gang youth occupying the territory almost didn't let him pass, thinking he was an undercover cop. Sy saw Judy as a magician who could shift neighborhood youth from vandalizing parks to beautifying them. When he asked, "How do we make this thing work in a broader scale?" Judy replied that he could pay her to create murals with youth, rather than teach classes at recreation centers. Sy appointed her director of the Eastside Murals.

Her work also caught the attention of gangs. One, the White Fence Gang of Boyle Heights, called the mayor's office asking for the "mural lady" to help them paint a mural. Painters working on her next mural, titled *Medusa Head*, on a wall of the Wabash

Community Center included members of the White Fence Gang. The Medusa's head was painted on the double doors at the entrance. Sprouting from it were flowery vines that climbed up the walls of the building.

"While I could move between the parks, my new friends could not travel even a mile to a neighboring park for fear of reprisals by rival neighborhood gangs," Judy said of the challenge of bringing youth from warring neighborhood gangs together. Amazingly it was her mural project that succeeded. Boundaries between youth relaxed as they identified and bonded as muralists.

One of her main artists, Jorge, had decorated a neighborhood garage door with graffiti. Now he was using his talent to paint a startling image on a public building. He encouraged fellow members of the Evergreen Gang, also from Boyle Heights, to join in. Together they collaborated with Fernando, a member of another gang who had worked with Judy on a previous mural.

As a friend and teacher of gang youth, Judy mourned with the family of one of her designers who was killed in gang violence. From 3 PM to late into the night Judy's world was in East Los Angeles working with youth. The remainder of her time, living in the beach town of Venice where she rented an apartment, was a totally different existence. The male artists who dominated the art scene in East L.A. were unwilling to treat Judy as an equal. They didn't consider her art as important as theirs. Her landlady introduced her to a blossoming feminist community where Judy found support as she explored her womanhood in discussion groups with women doctors, lawyers, scientists, artists, and other professionals. Christina Schlesinger, a young artist who volunteered on the mural project, became an important partner in Judy's work.

Judy soon made her project citywide to garner more support from the city politicians. Along with success came more and more responsibilities but barely any increase in funding. Judy now oversaw 40 mural projects a year. Each community, whether it was L.A.'s Koreatown or the city's Thai neighborhood, required different skills. Now she was working with everyone from nuns to criminals. As communities took ownership of their projects the murals focused on the serious issues of drug abuse, immigration, and police brutality, unleashing complaints from some citizens.

"I was stuck between the city and the community. And at both ends I was despised—the community, because they saw me as being part of the city; the city, because they saw me being a community person and a radical." The endless hours and conflicts with the city and with communities took their toll. Judy became ill and was headed for a nervous breakdown. Her cure was a trip to Mexico with Christina to view murals by Mexican masters.

When Judy returned from Mexico, she formed an advisory committee of influential people interested in the project, and they became devoted to safeguarding the communities' creations. Two lawyers on the committee offered to help her incorporate a nonprofit organization called SPARC, the Social and Public Art Resource Center. Cofounded in 1976 with artist Christina Schlesinger and filmmaker Donna Deitch, this new organization gave Judy and her coworkers more freedom to raise funds and organize new murals. Two years earlier Judy had been contacted by the US Army Corps of Engineers about creating a mural on the 2,754-foot concrete wall lining the corps' Tijunga Flood Control Channel in San Fernando Valley. Now that Judy had the backing of SPARC she could accept their invitation to embark on such a long-term project. If the city dropped funding, SPARC could help her continue her work.

"When I first saw the wall, I envisioned a long narrative of another history of California; one which included ethnic

peoples, women, and minorities who were so invisible in con-
ventional textbook accounts," Judy reminisced.

This ambitious project—a more than half-mile-long pictorial
history of the people's history of California—would be not only
grand in scale but in participation. Over the many years it took
to complete, Judy employed more than 400 young people and
their families from diverse ethnic and economic backgrounds
who worked with dozens of professional artists, historians, eth-
nologists, and community supporters. Started while Judy was
overseeing the City's Mural Project, from the third year on it
became a project of SPARC.

Starting with California's prehistory, the mural achieved
Judy's dream of depicting a more accurate history of the state
from early years to present. Many of the scenes contradict the
school textbook version of the state's past. The commonly told
tale of how the Spanish founded Los Angeles was turned on its
head by artwork showing that the majority of the 22 people in
the expedition were mulatto, black, mestizo, or Indian. The
section on Gold Rush history with images of black, Mexican,
Indian, and Chinese miners dominated a period of history often
pictured with bearded, white, male miners. Also unveiled were
Thomas Edison's rumored Mexican heritage and the story of
the death of Dr. Charles Drew, the black inventor of lifesaving
blood plasma, who died in a Southern hospital where he had
been refused treatment because of his race.

After returning from Mexico in 1977, Judy incorporated
muralist David Alfaro Siquieros's concept of the musical ratio
into her design of *Great Wall*. Using his design formula she
smoothly integrated the artwork created by her team of artists.
Supervising a mural of this size was like directing a major movie
production. Procuring paint, setting up scaffolds, providing
food for all the workers, assigning tasks, working out conflicts,

and teaching painting skills kept Judy on the run. By 1980, 600 gallons of paint and 65,000 kid-hours had been expended on the project. Even before *Great Wall* was completed in 1983, it had broken the record for the longest mural in the world.

During her years overseeing the creation of *Great Wall* Judy returned to Mexico for an intensive mural workshop in which she was the sole female student among the other 30-plus participants. During this same period she returned to Cal State Northridge to earn a master's degree in art education. In 1980 Judy began her career as a professor at the University of California, first at the Irvine campus and then at UCLA where she cofounded the Cesar Chavez Center and the UCLA SPARC César Chávez Digital/Mural Lab in 1996. At Judy's lab, housed at SPARC, she developed digital techniques for creating murals, as well as innovative hands-on training for university students and artists working with communities in the creating of murals.

Since her mural work first began, Judy has worked on 3,000 projects. In 1987 she embarked on the ambitious work, *The World Wall: A Vision of the Future Without Fear*, an artwork showing a world without violence. Other artists from around the world added panels that then traveled around the world. Each year Judy's murals sprouted in public sites, from government buildings to schools and freeway bridges throughout Los Angeles. She was commissioned to create murals in cities in California, Colorado, and Texas, as well as the Central American nation of El Salvador. Year after year, one organization after another honored her for her efforts, but creating and protecting existing murals started to become an issue after the turn of the 21st century.

Since 2008 Judy and fellow supporters of public art have been fighting the destruction of murals and working to restore damage to murals like *Great Wall* caused by pollution. As much as Judy has accomplished, her goals remained the same as she neared her 70th birthday.

"I hope to use public space to create public voice, and consciousness about the presence of people who are often the majority of the population but who may not be represented in any visual way," says Judy. "By telling their stories we are giving voice to the voiceless and visualizing the whole of the American story while creating sites of public memory."

LEYMAH GBOWEE

———◆———

Women in White Demand Peace

"Do peace and justice at home. Do peace and justice in your backyard. And spread your experiences outside."
                                                    —*Leymah Gbowee*

A s rebel forces neared their home in the outskirts of Monrovia, Liberia's capital, Leymah Gbowee and her family fled to the dormitory at their church in the city. There they were safe until one morning when government soldiers barged inside and ordered everyone to line up outdoors. One soldier ordered a woman who was sobbing uncontrollably to be silent; her sister told him to leave her alone. In return the soldier slapped her. After she slapped him back, he shot her dead.

Leymah feared for her life, but for the moment she was safe because her family spoke Mende, the same language the soldiers used. The soliders let the group in the church go with the warning that the next group of soldiers might not be so "nice." That night Leymah and her family moved into the tiny apartment where her sister's fiancé lived. The following day news came that several hundred members of the Gio and Mano tribes who had sought sanctuary at the church had been massacred by another battalion of soldiers.

This was the beginning of Leymah's journey, amid violence and the unknown, to becoming a force for peace.

Leymah's father, a radio operator, was 10 years older than her mother; she gave birth to their first daughter, Geneva, soon after their marriage. Next came another daughter, Josephine. Hoping for a boy, their mother was disappointed when she gave birth to a third daughter on February 1, 1972. Demonstrating her frustration and questioning why she did not bear a son, she named her baby Leymah, meaning, "What is it about me?" Leymah's father, however, called her his "luck child" because he landed a good job with the Liberian government's security agency just

LIBERIAN HISTORY

Liberia has been rife with class tensions from the start. Settlers, mainly freed slaves from the United States and Africans liberated from slave ships, colonized part of Africa's West Coast and established Liberia in 1847. Ironically the ex-slaves became masters of the indigenous tribal people, claiming both political and economic power.

after her birth. Later he was promoted to chief radio technician, and her mother became a pharmacist.

With the arrival of two more daughters, Mala and Fata, Leymah's parents had their hands full, but with their good jobs they had the money to buy land outside of Monrovia. They built a house, bought a car, and sent their daughters to private schools.

Leymah was an ambitious student. Her father would tell her, "I know one day you will be great." After being hospitalized twice at the age of 13 for an ulcer and enduring bouts of malaria and cholera, she set her sights on becoming a doctor.

Soon any hope for Leymah's future plans evaporated. While she celebrated her graduation from high school, armed rebels under the leadership of Charles Taylor entered Liberia from Côte d'Ivoire to overthrow President Samuel Doe. As Leymah began her studies at the University of Liberia, rebels were bringing down her country's government.

Her parents, who had moved to a new home on a bigger plot of land in Paynesville, a suburb of Monrovia, paid little heed to reports of the rebel advance, but eldest daughter Geneva insisted they flee to neighboring Sierra Leone. Their father disagreed. Soon family members arrived in Paynesville as they fled fighting near their villages. Before long they heard gunfire as the rebels battled nearby. With no time to pack possessions, Leymah and her family abandoned their home. After the incident at the church, they wanted to keep on the move and sought safe haven in one place after another. Gone were the days when they could stroll down the avenues without having to view dead bodies or hide from unpredictably violent child soldiers. Before their eyes, Monrovia was being destroyed. Their father was still employed by the Liberian Security Agency, working and living at the US embassy, but he could not house them there. Knowing

SAMUEL DOE

In 1980 Samuel Doe, then an army sergeant, seized power from Liberian president William Tolbert, a member of the elite ruling class. Doe became the first president from a lower class. He executed Tolbert and members of his administration. People thought the installation of the first nonelite president might signal the end of the rigid class structure, but Doe turned out to be corrupt and violent. He stole millions and executed opponents. He favored people in his tribe, the Krahn, and he discriminated against others such as people of the Gio and Mano tribes. Now tribal identity started to matter.

it was time for his wife and children to leave, he secured passage for them on a ship to Sierra Leone. They boarded the vessel, which was jam-packed with refugees, and they were surprised to arrive instead in Accra, Ghana.

Along with hundreds of other displaced people, Leymah's family now lived crammed together in an unfinished one-room concrete house at a refugee camp. They had no idea when they could return home. Leymah lived in a daze. "I saw no future at all; for me time had stopped," she wrote.

In May 1991 they heard news that an African peacekeeping force (ECOWAG) had arrived in Monrovia to stop the fighting and help set up an interim government. Leymah's sister

Josephine had a newborn child to care for. Though her husband was in Monrovia, she felt safer at the camp. Leymah, with no reason to stay, convinced her mother to let her go home. Returning to Liberia was a shock.

"The port smelled of death and destruction, and my first glimpse of Monrovia almost took my breath away." She shared an apartment with her sister Josephine's husband and a couple of friends. Leymah enrolled in typing school. She wanted to get back on track, but there were no jobs. The university was closed. The city was in shambles. Without school or work, Leymah became listless.

It was in this state of mind that she fell prey to a Ghanaian named Daniel. He pursued and charmed her. Though Leymah

CHILD SOLDIERS

The use of children, primarily boys, as soldiers has occurred for thousands of years. Typical roles in the past were as drummer boys, spies, lookouts, messengers, and porters. During the second half of the 20th century, children were also used as foot soldiers armed with automatic weapons. In Cambodia and many African countries child soldiers were desensitized to killing through use of drugs that enabled them to commit mass killings of civilians. Despite international laws banning the use of child soldiers, as of 2015 they were in use in at least five countries.

sensed danger she lapsed into dependency. He had money and was always there to help. By the time he started to physically abuse her, she was pregnant. Following the birth of her little boy, Nuku, she had two more children, Amber and Arthur. For the next few years her life was grim as she suffered domestic abuse and extreme poverty. The family once again fled to Ghana to avoid an outbreak of violence. Day by day Daniel's abuse eroded her dignity. It was at the lowest point that Leymah found the strength to leave Daniel and return to Liberia. "I was twenty-six, penniless, broken, and charged with the care of three utterly dependent toddlers. Soon to be four." She gave birth to her fourth child, Pudu, while living with her parents in Paynesville.

Back in Monrovia, Leymah slowly began to recover as she volunteered for the Trauma Healing and Reconciliation Program (THRP) sponsored by her church. She enrolled at Mother Patern College to earn a degree in social work. As she learned how to help people recover from war traumas, she started healing as well. By encouraging villagers to tell their stories she enabled them to let go of painful experiences. By asking them questions about resolving conflicts in their communities, she gave them power to rebuild relationships with those who wronged them.

Recovery wasn't instant. It came step by step, just as Leymah rebuilt her self-image bit by bit. On trips to villages Leymah grieved with women who had lost their homes or their children, and those who had been raped. Her boss and coworkers were impressed by her ability to help people open up. Leymah's work soon evolved from self-therapy into a passion. Her coworkers changed from strangers to family. She became close with an American named Jill, who, after returning home to Chicago, mailed Leymah money for school fees.

Leymah worked long hours each day, working at THRP, attending classes, doing homework, and caring for her children. She loved being in school again and feeling challenged at work. She took on the task of helping boy soldiers to heal from the trauma of committing horrible atrocities. Her unflinching manner in response to their threats and taunts earned her the title "the General." Leymah was discovering powers that had been dormant. Soon she would be a general of a new kind of army.

Leymah moved with her children into her own apartment with her sister Geneva and her six-year-old niece, Leemu. She met Sam Doe, the founder the West Africa Network for Peacebuilding (WANEP) at work when he met with her boss to discuss WANEP's program of using nonviolent strategies in response to violence, war, and human rights abuses. In 1999 she was invited to the WANEP conference in Ghana where she found a new mission as she listened to presenters discuss peace-building principles. If she could help prevent or stop wars, people would not suffer traumas and need the healing that she was providing. Realizing how much women bore the tragedies of war, Leymah became convinced that women, more than men, should be peace builders, and she could be one of them.

Leymah often told trauma victims, "You are in the Valley of Misery, a place of anger, depression, and hurt. The person who hurt you . . . is also here . . . if you haven't been able to forgive, you are chained to him." Following her own advice, before going home from the conference in Ghana she visited Daniel to forgive him and let go of her anger.

Leymah met Thelma Ekiyor, a dynamic Nigerian lawyer, at the next conference. Thelma shared her dream of starting a women's peace-building group modeled after WANEP. In the summer of 2001 Leymah graduated from Mother Patern and was hired full-time at THRP. The West Africa Network for

Peacebuilding had awarded Thelma funds to start her dream organization, Women in Peacebuilding Network (WIPNET), and she invited Leymah to help launch the network at a conference in Accra. With enthusiasm Leymah took on one task after another. Seeing her leadership potential, Thelma appointed Leymah as the WIPNET coordinator in Liberia. Up until now, the group advocating for women's issues in Liberia had been composed of women from the elite class. Many of them did not want to support a new organization, especially with someone of Leymah's background in charge. However, Etweda "Sugars" Cooper, the godmother of the Liberian women's movement, had heard of Leymah's work at THRP and offered her full support.

Just as Leymah started recruiting and training women as peacemakers, fighting broke out once more. Leymah wondered if she should bundle up her children and leave for the safety of Ghana. This would mean quitting her jobs. Her sister Geneva promised to take the children and care for them in Accra while Leymah stayed in Liberia. She persuaded Leymah that not only was her work important but also that they needed the money. So while Geneva looked after the children in Ghana, Leymah labored during the day for THRP, and for WIPNET at night.

What helped her through the long hours was the memory of a session at a refugee camp. The intensity of women telling tales of one atrocity after another prompted Leymah to say, "We can stop. It's okay." An old woman stood up saying that the session was more valuable than food, shelter, and clothes. "Please don't stop," she said. "Don't ever stop." This became Leymah's mantra.

One night she had a dream in which a voice told her to "Gather the women and pray for peace." Leymah assembled Christian women, and a Women in Peacebuilding Network leader named Asatu rallied her fellow Muslim women. As Charles Taylor restricted freedoms and violence increased, Leymah launched the Peace Outreach Project. She and WIPNET volunteers handed out flyers that said, "We are tired! We are tired of our children being killed! We are tired of being raped! Women wake up—you have a voice in the peace process!"

By the summer of 2002, Leymah and her "peace women," as they were now known, inaugurated the Women of Liberia Mass Action for Peace to amplify their message. Each day women, both Christian and Muslim, gathered at the fish market to sing and pray. That winter they shocked Monrovia by marching in solidarity to city hall, where Leymah spoke of their vision for peace before a large crowd.

It had been 13 years of off-and-on-again war. It was time for women to end the fighting. Leymah rallied hundreds of women, dressed in white T-shirts and white headscarves, to assemble in a field bordering the road that Charles Taylor traveled twice a day from his mansion to Capitol Hill. Day after day, regardless of intense heat or pouring rain, they were there demanding a meeting with Taylor to talk of peace. He finally invited them to come to the executive mansion on April 23, 2003.

Leymah now had to muster the courage to stand before a murderous tyrant and make her plea. That day more than 2,000 women assembled outside while Leymah stood bravely before the peace women, legislators, and Taylor, and said, "We are now taking this stand to secure the future of our children. Because we believe as custodians of society, tomorrow our children will ask us, 'Mama, what was your role during the crisis?'"

Taylor agreed to hold peace talks if the women requested the same of the rebels. Several of the peace women met with the rebels. By scolding them on behalf of their mothers and sisters, and appealing to their egos by saying that the country depended on important men like them to bring peace, the women convinced them to come to the peace table. In June 2003 Leymah and her troops arrived in Ghana to maintain pressure on the negotiators, who were meeting at a luxury hotel. The chief negotiator, General Abdulsalami Abubakar, a former president of Nigeria, had made a habit of stopping to chat with them, and he indicated he was on their side. After weeks of peacefully demonstrating, no progress had been made in the talks, and fighting continued in Liberia.

Reports of increasing violence at home, paired with the sight of rebel leaders lounging at the hotel bar, pushed Leymah over the edge. Reinforcements were bussed in from Liberian refugee camps to join her veteran forces. Linking their arms together

Leymah Gbowee with First Lady Michelle Obama, Secretary of State Hillary Clinton, and fellow 2011 Nobel Peace Prize laureate Tawakkol Karman.
Official White House Photo / Pete Souza

they blocked the exits from the meeting room. Leymah relayed a message to General Abubakar that the delegates were being held hostage so that they might suffer as the Liberian people were suffering. "The peace hall has been seized by General Leymah and her troops!" announced Abubakar over the loudspeaker.

When security guards arrived to arrest Leymah, she was so indignant that she threatened to strip off her clothes to make it easier. The men stood aghast as Leymah slowly disrobed. In most of Africa it is considered a curse when a married or elderly woman purposely bares herself. That day the peace women broke the deadlock. By August 18, 2003, a peace pact was in place.

Crowds cheered when the peace women returned home, but they knew their work was far from done. To keep the peace they needed to heal the rifts between opposing sides. They needed to support their people in rebuilding their country. After 14 years of war 250,000 people had died, 350,000 had lost their homes, and 1 million were so malnourished they were at risk of dying.

As Leymah worked with her WIPNET colleagues for a lasting peace, she earned a master's degree in peace building and assisted in the making of a documentary film, *Pray the Devil Back to Hell*, about their peace campaign. Leymah, not yet 40 years old, had faced serious personal as well as national struggles. What carried her through these times was an unerring faith in the future. In 2011 she received the Nobel Peace Prize along with Liberian president Ellen Sirleaf and Yemeni activist Tawakkol Karman. That same year she published her autobiography, *Mighty Be Our Powers*. The following year she established the Gbowee Peace Foundation to help the world find more roads to peace. In 2014 Leymah was still standing in the forefront of the effort to rebuild her country, this time through making sure people knew about how to avoid the threats of the Ebola virus.

RESOURCES

ORGANIZATIONS TO EXPLORE IN
PERSON OR ONLINE

American Friends Service Committee (AFSC)
www.afsc.org
Founded in 1917, the AFSC is a Quaker organization open to
people of all faiths working together to overcome injustice and
violence. Programs throughout the world focus on economic
and social justice, youth, peace building, and demilitarization.

Alice Paul Institute
www.alicepaul.org
Housed in Alice Paul's birthplace, Paulsdale, the Alice Paul
Institute is a nonprofit organization dedicated to carrying on
Alice's work to make gender equality a reality under the law.
The Alice Paul Leadership Program (APLP) educates adolescent
girls about accomplished women leaders of the past and pres-
ent to serve as role models for girls as they develop their own

leadership styles, and the program offers skill- and confidence-building exercises needed to become a leader in winning rights for women.

American Civil Liberties Union (ACLU)
www.aclu.org
This nonpartisan nonprofit organization is dedicated to defending and preserving rights of individuals and the liberties guaranteed to every person in this country by the Constitution and laws of the United States.

Child Labor Coalition
www.stopchildlabor.org
With the mission of ending child labor exploitation and insuring the health, safety, and education of working minors, this coalition of more than 25 organizations sheds light on abuses against child laborers throughout the world. Rich with information on every topic from the history of child labor to statistics, laws, and enforcement, this is a one-stop site for learning about child labor and campaigns to stop abuses.

Equal Rights Amendment.org
www.equalrightsamendment.org
A collaboration of the National Council of Women's Organizations and the Alice Paul Institute, this website provides information about the ERA and campaigns for its passage. Links are provided to numerous organizations, historical sites, and documents.

Gray Panthers
www.graypanthers.org
Find out more about Maggie Kuhn and the organization she

helped establish to support the rights of young and old alike through campaigns for single-payer health care, protection of programs for elders, economic security of all citizens, and civil rights. Join them in exposing lies about important social programs by fighting "truth decay." This site is peppered with clever Maggie "Kuhnisms" such as "The best age is the age you are."

Fellowship of Reconciliation (FOR)
www.forusa.org
FOR's intent is to substitute war, violence, racism, and economic injustice with nonviolence, peace, and justice through coalitions, training, and compassionate acts.

Gulabi Gang
http://gulabigang.in
This online forum offers videos, photos, and more information about the organization that Sampat Pal established in 2006 to demand justice for women in Uttar Pradesh, one of India's most impoverished regions.

International Labor Rights Forum
www.laborrights.org
Since the 1980s ILRF has been a vital player in bringing about solutions regarding issues and problems of worker rights and labor standards around the world.

League of Women Voters
www.lwv.org
Founded in 1920, the league was established to support women in using their new right to vote. Though it refrains from supporting a particular political party, it campaigns for voting

rights, which may be supported by one particular party. Among its key issues are making voter registration simple and accessible to all, insuring fair elections, educating voters, and reducing the influence of big money in election campaigns.

Malala Fund
www.malalafund.org
Due to political, religious, financial, or other reasons, 600 million adolescent girls around the world are denied the opportunity to attend school. Find out how to join Malala Yousafzai in helping every girl to get a formal education.

National Women's Hall of Fame
www.greatwomen.org
At this site are short biographies of American women noted for great achievements in a wide variety of fields, including many who worked alongside Alice Paul, Ida B. Wells, Margaret Sanger, and Jane Addams.

Peace Action
www.peace-action.org
Peace Action is devoted to abolishing nuclear weapons, ending the international weapons trade, and creating a peace-oriented economy.

Planned Parenthood Federation of America
www.plannedparenthood.org
In 1916 Margaret Sanger and others opened the first birth control clinic and the American Birth Control League began. In 1942 the organization changed its name to Planned Parenthood Federation of America to continue its work in educating and offering services about women's reproductive health, including

birth control and abortions. Today a network of Planned Parenthood groups throughout the United States operate clinics and provide educational materials and consultation on reproductive health, birth control, abortions, relationships, sexual orientation, sexuality, and a wide range of other sexual issues. Defending reproductive rights continues to be a major mission.

SPARK Movement
www.sparksummit.com
This site provides the latest information about the campaigns of SPARK team activists under the guidance of director Dana Edell. Also found here are a blog, information on becoming a member, and bios and contacts for SPARK team leaders. This is the place to add your name to petitions and find out about dozens of partner organizations, such as Ma'yan and iOppose.

Yellowberry
www.yellowberrycompany.com
This site is the online home for Megan Grassell's company, Yellowberry, featuring a variety of bra styles for girls 11 to 15. Also included is a page about Megan, her philosophy, and her comments about creating Yellowberry.

Young Women's Christian Association (YWCA)
www.ywca.org
With more than 2 million members, the YWCA is one of the oldest and largest organizations devoted to improving women's lives and their communities. With its current motto "Eliminating racism, empowering women," the "Y" continues its historic mission of being in the forefront of social change. The organization supports women's health and safety by advocating for affordable health care and campaigning for laws to halt violence

against women at home, on dates, and in the military. The "Y" also provides child care, health, financial, and job training, as well as promoting the STEM initiative to improve the performance of girls in the fields of technology, math, and science. Since 1906 the "Y" has provided educational programs for women about sex and reproductive health.

AUDIOVISUAL LINKS

"Dr. Vandana Shiva—Solutions to the food and ecological crisis facing us today"
www.youtube.com/watch?v=ER5ZZk5atlE

"Rigoberta Menchú Live at The Human Forum Part 1"
www.youtube.com/watch?v=yvnUEup1hC4

"Leymah Gbowee: Unlock the intelligence, passion, greatness of girls"
www.youtube.com/watch?v=QxkxcsrveLw

"Kalpona Akter, Bangladesh Labor Leader: Part I"
www.youtube.com/watch?v=PouBiSZqDVo

"The Great Wall of Los Angeles"
www.youtube.com/watch?v=nM4CFBwj9fc

NOTES

Megan Grassell: Ripening a Yellowberry

"One of the biggest problems": "Yellowberry Founder Megan Grassell's Business Crash Course."

"Water the flowers": www.yellowberrycompany.com.

"I worked every summer since": "Yellowberry Founder."

"I couldn't believe the bras": Richard, "Yellowberry: Meet the Teen Titan Who Is Taking on the Youth Bra Industry," www.lingerietalk.com/2014/04/08/lingerie-news/yellowberry-meet-the-teen-titan-who-is-taking-on-the-youth-bra-industry.html.

"This company is my effort": www.yellowberrycompany.com.

"She came to me and said": Claire Martin, "Can't Find it at the Mall? Make it Yourself," *New York Times*, May 10, 2014.

"I didn't care how many adults chuckled": www.yellowberrycompany.com/ABUS.html.

Margaret Sanger: "Woman Must Not Accept; She Must Challenge"

"*I was resolved to seek out*": *Margaret Sanger: A Life of Passion*, 50.
"*I resolved that women should have*": *Sanger*, 50.
"*an enemy of the young*": *Sanger*, 70.
"*A woman's body belongs*": *Sanger*, 83.
"*Jail has not been my goal*": *Sanger*, 89.
"*beacons of light for*": *Sanger*, 133.

Alice Paul: Equal Rights for Women

"*I have never doubted*": www.voteera.org.
"*How can you dine*": *A Woman's Crusade: Alice Paul and the Battle for the Ballot*, 30.
"*mild-mannered girl*": *Crusade*, 5.
"*heart and soul convert*": *Crusade*, 23.
"*The police grabbed the suffragettes*": *Crusade*, 22.
Alice told her mother she was coming home: *Crusade*, 35.
Her major professor commented on the "*brilliance of her mind*": *Crusade*, 42.
"*What will you do*": *Crusade*, 148.
"*We the women of America*": *Crusade*, 172.

Maggie Kuhn: Young and Old Together

"*Old age is an excellent time for outrage*": www.graypanthers.org.
"*Young lady, do you have something to say?*": *No Stone Unturned: The Life and Times of Maggie Kuhn*, 145.
"*Sheer Luck*": *No Stone Unturned*, 71.
her forced retirement would be called "*the most significant*": *Maggie Growls* website, www.pbs.org/independentlens/maggiegrowls/film.html.
"*We felt at one with the young war*": *No Stone Unturned*, 131.
"*Our new name*": *No Stone Unturned*, 138.
"*Go to the top—that's my advice*": *No Stone Unturned*, 159.

Maggie took on the job of chief myth buster: www.graypanthers.org.
"pervasive put-downs": No Stone Unturned, 162.
"heal and humanize our society": www.graypathers.org.
"Don't agonize, organize": Maggie Growls website.
"amazing, canny, lusty, charming, and unstoppable": Maggie Growls website.
"Every one of us": No Stone Unturned, 152.

Sampat Pal Devi: Founding the Gulabi Gang

"Village society in India is loaded": Soutik Biswas, "India's 'Pink' Vigilante Women," BBC News, http://news.bbc.co.uk/2/hi/south_asia/7068875.stm.
"I was a happy girl": Warrior in a Pink Sari: The Inside Story of the Gulabi Gang as Told to Anne Berthod, 7.
"Stop bothering your daughter": Warrior in a Pink Sari, 15.
"Never let anyone hurt you": Warrior in a Pink Sari, 17.
"Suddenly the world": Warrior in a Pink Sari, 47.
"We are not a gang": "India's 'Pink' Vigilante Women."
"I have been a fighter": Rajesh Kumar Singh, "Gulabi Gang Opposes Chief Sampat Pal's Political Aspirations," *Lucknow Kindustan Times*, March 7, 2015.

Dana Edell: Girl Power

"How we are represented": Seher Ali, "Where We Belong: On the Status of Women in the US Media," www.sparksummit.com/2014/02/25%20where-we-belong-on-the-status-of-women-in-the-us-media.
"These photoshopped images": Carina Cruz and Emma Stydahar, "Teen Vogue: Give Us Images of Real Girls!," www.change.org/petitions/teen-vogue-give-us-images-of-real-girls.
"We have news": Deborah Tolman, "SPARKing Change: Not Just One Girl at a Time," *Huffington Post*, May 10, 2012, www.huffingtonpost.com/deborah-l-tolman/sparking-change-not-just-_b_1506433.html.

"It was thrilling": Culley Schultz, "We Can SPARK Action: Costume Is Off Shelves," SPARKsummit.com, October 28, 2011, www.sparksummit.com/2012/03/20/we-can-spark-action -costume-is-off-shelves.

"Seventeen listened!": "Teen Vogue."

"When someone who": Georgia Luckhurst, "Role Model: An Interview with Jennie Runk," SPARKsummit.com, July 29, 2013, www.sparksummit.com/2013/07/29/role-model-an -interview-with-jennie-runk.

"Google Doodles have become": Celeste Montaño, "Google: Doodle Us!" SPARKsummit.com, February 27, 2014, www.spark summit.com/2014/02/27/doodleus.

One Harvard clinical psychologist: Austin Considine, "Say 'No' to Picture Perfect," *New York Times*, May 16, 2012.

Malala Yousafzai: Speaking Out for Girls' Education

"This is what my soul": Malala Yousafzai, "Malala Yousafzai: 'Our Books and Our Pens Are the Most Powerful Weapons,'" *Guardian*, July 12, 2013.

"We realize the importance": "'Our Books and Our Pens.'"

"Malala is as free as a bird": I Am Malala: The Girl Who Stood Up for Education and Was Shot by the Taliban, 55.

"Freedom is not worth having": I Am Malala, 58.

"This is not the way": I Am Malala, 122.

"You were the one": I Am Malala, 225.

"One child, one teacher": "'Our Books and Our Pens.'"

Mary Harris "Mother" Jones: The Queen of Agitators

"My address is like my shoes": The Autobiography of Mother Jones, Frontispiece.

"In 1867, a fever epidemic swept": Mother Jones: The Most Dangerous Woman in America, 12.

"Often while sewing": Mother Jones, 42.

"the most dangerous woman in America": Autobiography, 13.
"At five-thirty in the morning": Mother Jones, 120.
"Every day little children": Mother Jones, 71.
"Well I've got stock": Mother Jones, 72.
"We want time to play": Mother Jones, 71.
"voice whose call": Mother Jones, 199–200.
"She is indeed their mother": Mother Jones, 118.
"It was a cold, terrible place": Autobiography, 112.
In the US Senate, she had been called: Mother Jones, 118.
"And I long to see the day": "Mother Jones Speaks," www.youtube
.com/watch?v=84vSVvaGsE4.
"Pray for the Dead": Mother Jones, 41.

Vandana Shiva: Food and Forests for the People

"You do not measure the fruit of your actions": David Ferguson,
"Anti-GMO Activist Vandana Shiva: 'Find the right thing to
do. That is your duty.'" Raw Story, June 14, 2012.
"Brothers! This forest is the source": "Gaura Devi 1925–1991,"
MountainShepherds.com, http://mountainshepherds.com
/about/chipko-heritage.
"She has always been a major influence": "Vandana Shiva—
Progressive."
"The statement that this kind of piracy": Scott London, "In the
Footsteps of Ghandi: An Interview with Vandana Shiva,"
www.scottlondon.com/interviews/shiva.html.
"The farmer suicides started": George Lerner, "Activist: Farmer
Suicides in India Linked to Debt, Globalization," CNN.com,
January 5, 2010, www.cnn.com/2010/WORLD/asiapcf
/01/05/india.farmer.suicides.
"The poorest families": "Progressive," 6.
"All members of the earth community": Earth Democracy: Justice, Sus-
tainability, and Peace, 10.
"I do have fun": "Progressive," 8.

Rigoberta Menchú Tum: Touched by the Hand of Destiny

"What I treasure": "Nobel Peace Laureates Rigoberta Menchú Tum,"http://peacejam.org/laureates/Rigoberta-Menchú-Tum -10.aspx.

"I remember it": I, Rigoberta Menchu: An Indian Woman in Guatemala, 41.

"hatred is a disease": "Rigoberta Menchu Live at the Human Forum," www.youtube.com/watch?v=yvnUEup1hC4&list =PLS049xtyDTzVcOFZbmhxJz-N6s3h8XDJN.

"We have broken the silence": "A Maya Quiché Woman Testifies," Women in World History, www.womeninworldhistory.com /contemporary-08.html.

"We need justice": "Nobel Laureate Rigoberta Menchú Hails Genocide Conviction of Ex-Guatemalan Dictator Ríos Montt," transcript of interview, DemocracyNow.org, www .democracynow.org/2013/5/15/nobel_laureate_rigoberta _mench_hails_genocide.

"To be a light to others": Rigoberta Menchú's Facebook page, January 5, 2011, www.facebook.com/pages/Rigoberta-Menchu /146249775418439.

Kalpona Akter: Garment Workers in Solidarity

"If they had let me keep my": "Bangladeshi Garment Workers Fight Back," 5.

"American companies know": Sarah Stillman, "Death Traps: Bangladesh Garment-Factory Disaster," New Yorker, May 1, 2013, 3.

"I had never seen anything": "Garment Workers," 4.

"I was born a second time": "Garment Workers," 4.

Pope Francis described the pay scale: "Garment Workers," 4.

"I don't want to": Sarah Stuteville, "'End Death Traps' Tour Puts Face on Garment Work in Bangladesh," Seattle Times, April 26, 2013.

"I am sure you are aware": mperry, "Bangladesh Worker Safety Activist Kalpona Akter Speaks at Walmart Shareholder

Meeting," http://makingchangeatwalmart.org/2013/06/07
/bangladesh-worker-safety-activist-kalpona-akter-speaks
-at-walmart-shareholder-meeting.

Jane Addams: Weaving the Safety Net, Joining Hands for Peace

"*The public and government*": *Jane Addams: Spirit in Action*, 102.

"*My dear Double-D-'ed Addams*": From *Nobel Lectures, Peace 1926– 1950*, Frederick W. Haberman, ed. (Elsevier Publishing Company: Amsterdam, 1972), via "Jane Addams - Biographical," Nobelprize.org, Nobel Media AB 2014, February 2015, www.nobelprize.org/nobel_prizes/peace/laureates/1931/addams-bio.html.

"*always be honest with yourself*": *Spirit in Action*, 63.

"*I felt that this passive resistance of mine*": *Twenty Years at Hull House: With Autobiographical Notes*, 57.

"*It is so free of 'professional doing good'*": *Spirit in Action*, 63.

"*great reservoirs of human ability*": *Spirit in Action*, 138.

Ida B Wells: Shining the Light on Lynching

"*I'd rather go down in history*": *Crusade for Justice: The Autobiography of Ida B. Wells*, 370.

"*poor teachers whose mental*": *Crusade*, 36.

"*There is therefore only one thing*": *Crusade*, 72.

"*Nobody in this section of the country*": *Crusade*, 43.

"*Anyone attempting to publish the paper again*": *Crusade*, 43.

"*My duties as editor*": *Crusade*, 242–3.

"*only one social center welcomes the Negro*": *Crusade*.

Buffy Sainte-Marie: It Shines Through Her

"*I sang 'Now That the Buffalo Is Gone'*": *Buffy Sainte-Marie: It's My Way*, 153.

"*I was raised in a situation*": *Buffy Sainte-Marie*, 18.

"It wasn't possible to be": Buffy Sainte-Marie, 21.

"The Indians did not lose": Buffy Sainte-Marie, 39.

"In my own language [Cree] there": Brenda Norrell, "Beyond Images of Women and Indians: Straight-Talk from a Cree Icon," Censored blog, 1999, http://bsnorrell.tripod.com/id99.html.

"And he knows he shouldn't kill": www.buffysainte-marie.com/?page_id=789#us.

"If I lived till tomorrow": Buffy Sainte-Marie, 67.

"most scathing topical": Buffy Sainte-Marie, 65.

"There is a sense of royalty about": Buffy Sainte-Marie, 75.

"Indians still exist": "Biography," Indigenous Music Awards, http://aboriginalpeopleschoice.com/artists/buffy-sainte-marie/.

"We got the federal marshals": www.buffysainte-marie.com/page_id=757#bmhawk.

"It's futile to rush": Buffy Sainte-Marie, 258.

Judy Baca: Walls That Shout

"I was watching my cousins": Patt Morrison, "Judy Baca: Muralista," Los Angeles Times, August 28, 2010.

"The police called it a people's": To Sin Against Hope: How America Has Failed Its Immigrants: A Personal History, 100.

"I started to become": "Oral history interviews with Judith Baca, 1986 August 5–6," Archives of American Art, Smithsonian Institution, www.aaa.si.edu/collections/interviews/oral-history-interviews-judith-baca-5436.

"I had an understanding": "Muralista."

"I would draw these little": "Interviews with Judith Baca," 13.

"The police had been": Judith Baca, "The Art of the Mural," American Family: Journey of Dreams, www.pbs.org/americanfamily/mural.html.

"Gang Members Put Down": "Interviews with Judith Baca," 27.
"While I could move between the parks": "Art of the Mural."
"I was stuck between the city": "Interviews with Judith Baca," 41.
"When I first saw the": "The Great Wall of Los Angeles," www
.judybaca.com.
"I hope to use public space": "Biography," www.judybaca.com.

Leymah Gbowee: Women in White Demand Peace

"Do peace and justice at home": "Remarks by Leymah Gbowee,"
National Council of Churches, October 7, 2011, www.ncccusa
.org/news/111026gboweetranscript.html.
"I know one day": Mighty Be Our Powers: How Sisterhood, Prayer,
and Sex Changed a Nation at War, 13.
"I saw no future at all": Mighty Be Our Powers, 36.
"The port smelled of death and destruction": Mighty Be Our Powers,
37.
"I was twenty-six, penniless, broken": Mighty Be Our Powers, 69.
"You are in the Valley of Misery": Mighty Be Our Powers, 102.
"We can stop. It's okay": Mighty Be Our Powers, 121.
"Gather the women": Mighty Be Our Powers, 122.
"We are tired": Mighty Be Our Powers, 127.
"We are now taking this stand": Mighty Be Our Powers, 141.
"The peace hall has been seized": Mighty Be Our Powers, 161.

BIBLIOGRAPHY

INTERVIEWS

Telephone interview with Dana Edell, February 20, 2014.

Telephone interview with Megan Grassell, June 11, 2014.

Telephone interview with Julie J. Bryan about Maggie Kuhn, June 22, 2014.

BOOKS

Addams, Jane. *Twenty Years at Hull House: With Autobiographical Notes*. New York: Signet Classics, 1961.

Baker, Jean H. *Margaret Sanger: A Life of Passion*. New York: Hill and Wang, 2011.

Gbowee, Leymah. *Mighty Be Our Powers: How Sisterhood, Prayer, and Sex Changed a Nation at War*. New York: Beast Books, 2011.

Gorn, Elliot J. *Mother Jones: The Most Dangerous Woman in America*. New York: Hill and Wang, 2002.

Gutierrez, Alfredo. *To Sin Against Hope: How America Has Failed Its Immigrants: A Personal History*. Brooklyn: Verso Books, 2013.

Jones, Mother. *The Autobiography of Mother Jones.* Chicago: Charles H. Kerr & Co., 1925.

Knight, Louis W. *Jane Addams: Spirit in Action.* New York: W. W. Norton, 2010.

Kuhn, Maggie. *No Stone Unturned: The Life and Times of Maggie Kuhn.* New York: Ballantine, 1991.

Menchú, Rigoberta. *I, Rigoberta Menchu: An Indian Woman in Guatemala.* New York: Verso, 2010.

Pal, Sampat. *Warrior in a Pink Sari: The Inside Story of the Gulabi Gang as Told to Anne Berthod.* New Delhi: Zubaan, 2012.

Shiva, Vandana. *Stolen Harvest: The Hijacking of the Global Food Supply.* Cambridge, MA: South End Press, 2000.

Shiva, Vandana. *Earth Democracy: Justice, Sustainability, and Peace.* Cambridge, MA: South End Press, 2005.

Stonechild, Blair. *Buffy Sainte-Marie: It's My Way.* Markham, ON: Fifth House, 2012.

Walton, Mary. *A Woman's Crusade: Alice Paul and the Battle for the Ballot.* New York: Palgrave Macmillan, 2010.

Weatherford, Doris. *American Women's History.* New York: Macmillan, 1994.

Wells, Ida B. *Crusade for Justice: The Autobiography of Ida B. Wells.* Edited by Alfreda M. Duster. Chicago: University of Chicago Press, 1991.

Yousafzai, Malala, and Christina Lamb. *I Am Malala: The Girl Who Stood Up for Education and Was Shot by the Taliban.* Boston: Little Brown and Company, 2013.

MAGAZINES

Barsamian, David. "Vandana Shiva—Progressive." *Progressive.* September 1997.

Fontanella-Khan, Amana. "The Baddest Woman in India." *Slate.* August 13, 2013.

Goldberg, Michelle. "Awakenings: On Margaret Sanger." *Nation.* February 27, 2012.

Locker, Melissa. "Yellowberry Founder Megan Grassell's Business Crash Course." *Fortune.* April 22, 2014.

North, James. "Bangladeshi Garment Workers Fight Back." *Nation.* November 15, 2013.

Wareham, Dean. "Buffy Sainte-Marie Interviewed." *Magnet.* September 17, 2009.

INDEX